LILY

Reaktion's Botanical series is the first of its kind, integrating horticultural and botanical writing with a broader account of the cultural and social impact of trees, plants and flowers.

Published
Oak Peter Young
Geranium Kasia Boddy
Lily Marcia Reiss
Pine Laura Mason

Forthcoming
*Yew, Bamboo, Willow, Palm,
Orchid* and others

Lily

Marcia Reiss

REAKTION BOOKS

For Charlie

Published by
REAKTION BOOKS LTD
33 Great Sutton Street
London EC1V 0DX, UK

www.reaktionbooks.co.uk

First published 2013
Copyright © Marcia Reiss 2013

Printed and bound in China by C&C Offset Printing Co., Ltd

British Library Cataloguing in Publication Data
Reiss, Marcia.
Lily. – (Botanical)
1. Lilies.
I. Title II. Series
584.3-dc23

ISBN 978 1 78023 093 1

Contents

✣

Introduction: A Flower with Multiple Personalities

❧

I f the lily were a person, it would be diagnosed with multiple personality disorder. Its ever-changing story – in mythology, religion, art, literature and popular culture – is one of dramatic opposites: chastity vs sexuality; good vs evil; nurturing vs poisoning; life vs death. People have been married and buried with lilies for thousands of years. The myths of their origins are tales both of blood and mother's milk. Just when you think you know the lily, it surprises you.

The family of lilies is an extended clan of global diversity. It includes some 3,000 species and tens of thousands of hybrids, a number that increases every year. Lilies are the oldest cultivated flowers known to man. The tombs of the pharaohs are inscribed with images of lilies and the bulbs are cited in Chinese texts 2,000 years old. Lilies have played a part in the great gardens of the world, from the earthly paradises of Islam to the ordered perfection of Versailles and the naturalistic fantasies of vast English estates.

To tell their story is to speak of many different kinds of lilies from many different parts of the world. Botanically speaking, most lilies belong to one big family, Liliaceae, but some species have branched out into their own family groups, and others are lilies in name only. One of the oldest and best-known images of the lily, the fleur-de-lis (French for lily flower), looks more like an iris, and historians have debated for centuries which flower it truly represents. The biblical references to the lily are also widely divergent. They range from the

The Easter cover of the satirical magazine *Puck* (1910) is a humorous expression of the good and evil duality of lily symbolism.

sensual metaphors of the Song of Songs (also known as the Song of Solomon) – 'Your belly is a heap of wheat bordered with lilies' (4:3) – to the best-known phrase from Jesus' Sermon on the Mount: 'consider the lilies of the field' (Matthew 6:28). Are these today's Easter lilies, or the tiny lily of the valley, also mentioned in the Song of Songs

Ancient Egyptian
goddess with lily
sceptre, 3rd century
BC, limestone relief.

– 'I am the rose of Sharon and the lily of the valley' – or any number
of flowers also called lilies?

Sunday school texts aside, the biblical lily was not the familiar
white Easter lily. Botanists believe that it could have been one of
several lilies native to the Middle East, white, purple, even red. The
likely candidates, still found in the Mediterranean region, are part of
the largest group of lilies, classified as the *Lilium* genus. Known as
true lilies, the genus includes a huge variety of white and colourful
lilies common in today's gardens and florist shops. While this book
will focus on the true lilies, it will also consider other lilies of the
field – vivid bursts of daylilies, curvaceous calla lilies, mysterious
water lilies, tiny sprays of ground-hugging lilies of the valley and
several other species not nearly as well known. They have all inspired
herbalists, botanists, artists, poets, prophets, priests and storytellers
of every age.

Lilies and other flowers from *Fruits and Flowers from Bible Lands*, one of a set of cards published by the Religious Tract Society, England (1863).

Lilies are entwined with the basic elements of human life in cultures all over the world. They have been foraged in the wild and cultivated in gardens for food, medicine and cosmetics throughout the history of civilization. Women in ancient Egypt perfumed their bodies with oils extracted from lilies. Treasured for their fragrance and beauty and revered for their symbolic purity, lilies were valued just as much in medieval times for their use in treating a snakebite or a boil. As Victorian plant collectors trekked through East Asia in search of exotic lilies, they also discovered that the Chinese and Japanese had been eating these prized bulbs for centuries, just like potatoes. Roman legions had done the same with the bulbs of Madonna lilies and also used a poultice made from the bulbs to ease their sore feet.

From the Old and New Testaments to the Taj Mahal, lilies appear in the art and literature of Judaism, Christianity and Islam. They are literally the milk and blood of ancient myth and legend, conveying passion and fecundity in tales of life and death. In Greek mythology, lilies first sprouted on earth from drops of breast milk from the goddess Hera. In Christian legend, a dragon spilled the blood of St Leonard and lilies of the valley sprang up where the drops fell. From the earliest days of Christianity, the white lily became a symbol of the Virgin Mary's purity and blossomed centuries later as an iconic image in countless examples of Renaissance art.

By the nineteenth century religious symbolism had given way to a belief in the spiritual meaning of flowers. In the Victorian 'language of flowers', that romantic hotchpotch of historic and invented

Easter photo of a chick with a tiny wagon of lilies of the valley, *c.* 1908.

Watercolour painting, early 19th century, of a red lily detail from the Taj Mahal cenotaph. The centre lily is flanked by crown imperials, also known as Turkish lilies.

symbolism, white lilies still represented purity and innocence. But in the paintings of the Pre-Raphaelites, notably Dante Gabriel Rossetti, lilies took on a sensuous realism. Their meaning, as portrayed by many artists of this era, became increasingly complex, both religious and secular, at once innocent and erotic. The lily, not always white, was a favourite flower of the poet Emily Dickinson and of artists of the Aesthetic and Arts and Crafts movements. William Morris and Walter

Attributed to Melozzo da Forlì (1438–1494), *Annunciation*, fresco in the Chapel of the Annunciation, Pantheon, Rome. The angel Gabriel holds a lily, a sign of the Virgin Mary's purity.

Wallpaper design with lilies and doves by Walter Crane, 1876.

Crane wove them into their wallpaper designs and Oscar Wilde wore a lily on his lapel as a badge of his love of beauty. After Wilde's trial for sodomy, it became a sign of his homosexuality. One of Louis Comfort Tiffany's most intricate and expensive leaded glass lamps was named 'Pond Lily Descending'. But as Wilde had discovered, art for art's sake often came at a high price. The multicoloured lamp sold for the very expensive price of $400 in 1908, but it required time-consuming hand production and was discontinued after a few years.[1] During this period of artistic fascination with lilies, Frank Lloyd Wright created a water lily design for his art glass windows in 1895, and Claude Monet became obsessed with water lilies, creating 250 paintings of the flowers in his garden pond at Giverny.

After the white South African calla lily was introduced to the United States in the nineteenth century, it went through a gamut of symbolic transformations, from a mourning flower to an emblem of feminine beauty to a highly charged image of erotica. It was a provocative subject in early twentieth-century American art, a sexy immigrant that changed the lily's reputation. For painters from Georgia O'Keeffe to Salvador Dalí and photographers from Ansel Adams to Robert Mapplethorpe, the calla lily's sensual form was an irresistible subject. Some of their allusions are subtle, others can make you cringe. After looking at some of the graphically bold depictions by Dalí and Mapplethorpe, gardeners may find it hard to look a simple lily in the eye.

Lilies of all kinds have played a role in children's tales, such as the talking tiger lily in Lewis Carroll's *Through the Looking Glass* (1871), his sequel to *Alice's Adventures in Wonderland*. These and many others were wonderfully illustrated in children's books of the nineteenth century, most imaginatively by the Arts and Crafts artist Walter Crane. They are also closely associated with famous actors of the stage and screen. Lillie Langtry, a British nineteenth-century star and royal mistress, wore a signature lily in her hair and was known as the Jersey Lily. Katharine Hepburn's languid line in the film *Stage Door* (1937), 'The calla lilies are in bloom again', is still a famous refrain. Sidney Poitier won the Academy Award for best actor – the first for a black performer – for the film *Lilies of the Field* (1963). Lily metaphors have even found their way into everyday speech, from the tragedies of Shakespeare to the classic western movies of John Wayne.

Lilies evoke strong reactions. Some people hate them. The heady fragrance of a few varieties can be overpowering. 'In the garden of my childhood', the French novelist Colette recalled, the lilies' 'dazzling bloom and fragrance were lords of the garden'. But her mother, sitting inside the house, would call out to her: 'Shut the garden door . . .

those lilies are making the drawing room uninhabitable.'[2] A few species even stink. The smell of one, *Lilium amabile*, has been compared to 'a cross between an old tennis shoe and a rotted cabbage'. When B&D Lilies of Washington State first brought this species to flower, they 'thought something had crawled in under one of the greenhouse benches and died'. The nursery sells the bulb but advises one just to 'stand back and admire it for its beauty'.[3]

The brilliant colours of some hybrids can also offend those with more subdued tastes – or pronounced prejudices. In *My Garden Book*, the West Indian-born author Jamaica Kincaid, a passionate gardener, tells a tale of lilies that became a metaphor for racism. Walking through a friend's garden, she came upon a bed of brightly coloured Asiatic lilies and heard her friend's mother exclaim: 'Just look at these nigger colors!'[4] Even the pure white Madonna lily can conjure up conflicting sensations, at once innocent and sinister. Colette recalled her childhood memory of gathering them in sheaves to bring to the Virgin Mary's altar for the May crowning.

> The church was stuffy and hot, and the children were laden with flowers. The unruly smell of the lilies would grow thick and interfere with the singing of the hymns. Several of the faithful would get up and rush out; some would let their heads droop and then fall asleep, overcome by a strange drowsiness. But the plaster Virgin, standing on the altar, would be brushing with the tips of her dangling fingers the long, half-open cayman jaws of a lily at her feet.[5]

While Colette compares the lily's petals to the jaws of a cayman or crocodile, William Blake sees only innocent beauty:

> The modest Rose puts forth a thorn,
> The humble sheep a threat'ning horn:
> While the Lily white shall in love delight,
> Nor a thorn nor a threat stain her beauty bright.

'Lilies of All Kinds', drawing of anthropomorphic lilies by Walter Crane from
Flowers from Shakespeare's Garden (1906).

Georgia O'Keeffe said that she started thinking about calla lilies
'because people either liked or disliked them intensely'. While her
paintings caused a furore of reactions on both sides, she maintained:
'I had no feeling about them at all.'[6] Her paintings seem to indicate
otherwise. Love them or hate them, lilies have been a subject of fascination throughout the ages.

The prominent stamens and anthers of this white lily are features of the *Lilium* genus, known as true lilies.

one

A Lily by Any Other Name

Just what is a lily? Opening any garden book will send readers on a mind-boggling encounter. The index listings can be longer than for any other flower. And then there is the complex science of classification based on plant structure – not to mention all those Latin names. Here is a quick run-through of the system, which for the purposes of this book will be as simple as possible. Naming and grouping similar plants has been a human urge throughout history. Ancient scholars and herbalists in virtually every culture tried to make sense of their local flora, whether for medicine, food or beauty. The Greek philosopher and scientist Theophrastus (*c.* 371–287 BC) wrote voluminous botanical treatises, most of which survive today, establishing the first system of classifying plants. Two treatises written in the first century AD, by the Roman naturalist Pliny the Elder and the Greek physician Dioscorides, were accepted as botanical and even medical authorities until the nineteenth century. It has been claimed that Pliny, when describing a lily, was the first to use the word 'stamen' as it is used today, as the male element of the plant's reproductive system.[1] The names assigned to plants in ancient manuscripts would be debated and changed by botanists for centuries. While Latin names were ubiquitous, these tended to be subjective, based on individual ideas of which descriptive terms to include. Names for the same plant often differed and became long and unwieldy.

In the 1730s the Swedish botanist Carolus Linnaeus (1707–1778) called for a simpler system and created the one still in use today.

Simply put, he established binomial nomenclature, that is, giving each plant two Latin names, the first based on its genus and the second on its species. These terms are at the bottom of the hierarchy of plant classification, which starts with the kingdom. For true lilies, the order would be:

KINGDOM:	Plantae
DIVISION:	Monocotyledon
CLASS:	Liliopsida
ORDER:	Liliales
FAMILY:	Liliaceae
GENUS:	*Lilium*
SPECIES:	Approximately 110

One of the amazing things about lilies is their variety. The Liliaceae includes 250 genera, of which the largest is *Lilium*. The 110 species in this genus is a huge number. It may not seem that way, considering that the plant world has about 400,000 species. But the average genus has only eighteen species.[2] Linnaeus' list of plant names was published in 1753, and there have been many changes since then, not only additions but also reclassifications based on new discoveries about plant structure. Botanists over the centuries classified plants both by their flowers and by their seeds, roots and leaves. Today, DNA testing has provided more precise analyses, leading to even more reclassifications.

This book will use both common names and their established Latin binomials, as in tiger lily, first called *Lilium tigrinum*, now known as *Lilium lancifolium* because of its lance-like petals. The binomial's second name may be descriptive, as in *L. regale*, the regal lily, or editorial, as in *L. superbum*, a more flattering name for the American swamp lily. In other cases, it might refer to the name of the plant collector who discovered it, such as *L. henryi*, named for Augustine Henry, the Irish plant hunter who found this bright orange lily in China at the end of the nineteenth century, and Frank Kingdon-Ward, who discovered the tiny

L. occidentale, a wild lily found near the California and Oregon coast. Collectors nearly wiped out this colourful native in the mid-20th century and it is now officially identified as a rare and endangered plant.

L. wardii in the mountains of Tibet in 1924. Kingdon-Ward might be known today as an equal-opportunity collector: returning to Asia in 1946, he found the pink and white, bell-shaped *L. mackliniae* in Burma and named it for his wife, Jean Macklin.

The 110 *Lilium* species identified to date are the parents of the thousands of hybrid lilies available today, most of them created in the twentieth century. For this ever-increasing number of lily hybrids or cultivars, formed from crossing different species, just the cultivar name is used (without italics). Growers have given them some romantic monikers. Gardeners are much more likely to buy a lily called 'Enchantment' or 'Stargazer' than one described as a cross between two Latin binomials. In some cases, the names reflect the popular culture of the era in which they were coined. When Pieter Hoff, the largest lily grower in the Netherlands, was working on his family farm in the 1970s, he named most of his new lilies after songs by the rock band Santana, including 'Moonflower' and 'Black Magic Woman'.[3] Legions of amateur gardeners all over the world also hybridize lilies, practicing the art for their own pleasure and investing years to establish their seedlings as lasting cultivars. 'It's those first crosses that so easily can lead to a near addiction,' explains Charlie Kroell of Troy, Michigan, a self-described 'backyard pollen dauber'. 'Watching a new seedling of your own bloom for the first time is a thrill difficult to describe.'[4]

True Lilies, Relatives and Friends

True lilies, daylilies, lilies of the valley, calla lilies and water lilies have all played important roles in mythology, art, literature, horticulture and popular culture. In brief, here are their botanical biographies.

True lilies, the common name for the genus *Lilium*, include the best-known and most popular lilies, including the Easter lily and the Madonna lily — both have white trumpets but are considered different species. Like all members of the monocotyledon division, their seeds have only one seed leaf, or cotyledon. But like their monocot relatives the daffodil and the onion, they also grow from bulbs. True lily bulbs have fleshy scales, and unlike daffodils and onions, whose bulbs are protected by layers of papery skin, lily bulbs are never truly dormant and can dry out and die if not kept moist. Lily flowers display a great range of

L. canadense, also known as the Canada lily, is a tall, delicate species that grows from Alabama to Quebec. Discovered by the French settlers in Canada about 1620, it was one of the first North American lilies to reach Europe.

colour and form. They can be white, cream, pink, red, yellow or orange – in varying shades of every hue except blue and black. 'A true blue lily has been the Holy Grail of breeders from day one', according to hybridizer Charlie Kroell.[5] They can be flat or shaped like trumpets, bells or cups, face upright or hang downwards with reflexed or turned-back petals, known as Turk's caps. They all have a distinctive reproductive system consisting of a prominent pistil surrounded by six stamens, each with a large anther bearing brown or yellow pollen. The anthers swivel on the stamens, allowing maximum dispersal of pollen by insects, birds or the wind. The stems range in height from 8 inches to 8 feet (20 cm to 2.4 m). The leaves can be broad or grass-like, growing all along the stem, at times in overlapping whorls. Species lilies, the term for wild or native lilies, are found as far north as the Artic Circle and as far south as the Philippines and southern India, but most grow in the temperate zones of the northern hemisphere, mainly in eastern Asia and western North America, with a few in Europe and eastern North America. Most of the species lilies have either trumpet- or Turk's-cap-shaped flowers. DNA testing has revealed that these two types evolved independently, at least on three occasions in different countries.[6]

✸

Daylilies, or *Hemerocallis,* Greek for beauty of the day, were first considered a genus of the Liliaceae family but now constitute their own family, Hemerocallidaceae. They have lily-like flowers with six petals but can also be ruffled or spider-like. The blooms can stretch as wide as 5 inches (12.7 cm) across on bunches of stalks that can reach as high as 3 feet (91 cm). Rather than a true bulb, daylilies have crowns, the junction point from which their roots, stems and flowers grow. True to their name, the individual flowers last only a day, most blooming all day and some through the night. But there is a consolation to their 24-hour beauty: each flower stalk has several buds and each bunch has many stalks, so the flowering period can last several weeks. Native to Asia, they were introduced to Europe in the sixteenth century and have spread throughout both that continent and North

'Bali Watercolour' hybrid daylily with spider petals. Patrick Stamile, hybridizer; Michael Bouman, grower.

'Top of the Morning' hybrid daylily. Oscie Whatley, hybridizer; Michael Bouman, grower.

Orange daylily, Chinese painting of *Hemerocallis fulva*, 1813–40.

America. Most daylilies known today are sub-species of *Hemerocallis fulva*, the orange-coloured, ubiquitous plant that grows from a fleshy rhizome and forms long-lasting clumps with strap-like leaves. It can become weedy and has been disgraced as an invasive species called 'ditch lily' in some areas. But hybridizers, starting in Britain in 1877 and spreading with great enthusiasm to America, have restored its reputation as a highly desirable garden plant. In 1924 a bright pink variety of *H. fulva* was discovered in China and led to an explosion of multicoloured possibilities. Ten years later, A. B. Stout, the industry's legendary hybridizer, produced 'Theron', the first true red daylily.

Although daylilies never enjoyed the aristocratic reputation of true lilies – they were called 'wash-house lilies' in colonial America – thanks to modern hybridization they are being produced in an amazing array of colours and forms. The American Hemerocallis Society, founded in 1946, has been growing steadily and now has 8,000 members, including international producers from Australia to Zimbabwe. While it takes growers six years to ensure the characteristics of new cultivars, the strikingly beautiful results – and the continuing demand for them – make the effort worthwhile. Approximately 50,000 daylily cultivars have been developed, an impressive variety for a plant that was first known for only one colour and shape.

Lilies of the valley, native to temperate regions of the northern hemisphere, grow wild from Italy to Lapland and have naturalized in North America. This small genus was first placed in the Liliaceae family, but now has its own family group, Convallariaciae, named for the Latin word for valley, *convallaria.* Once called wood lilies, they were brought into English gardens about the middle of the sixteenth century but were often ignored by Renaissance botanists rediscovering more impressive plants from Greek and Roman texts. These ground-huggers, which spread by underground rhizomes, may be a lowly plant, but their colonies of tiny blooms have charmed people for centuries. Elizabethans collected unusual varieties with pink and red flowers. The most significant species, *Convallaria majalis,* is named for the Latin *maius,* meaning the month of May, the season when its tiny sprigs of white bell-like flowers with upturned edges stand within their own valley of broad leaves. They were gathered during Whitsuntide festivities in England and are still sold in France as good luck charms on 1 May. Although the plants are poisonous if eaten, old herbals recommend distilling them in wine to cure a wide range of ills.

opposite: A bunch of lilies of the valley.

Jacques Boyer, tendrils of lily of the valley, photograph, *c.* 1910.

A Paris vendor sells lilies of the valley, 1 May 1912, a first-of-May tradition throughout France.

Robert Mapplethorpe, *Calla Lily*, 1986. This photo and others by Mapplethorpe that focus on the calla lily's phallic spadix more graphically were featured in a controversial exhibition, 'The Perfect Moment', in 1989.

Calla lilies are known by different names, commonly as arum lilies and botanically as *Zantedeschia*, a name that few gardeners use and one that has little to do with the plant's origin or physical characteristics. It was introduced to Europe from South Africa in 1731, most likely from the Dutch colony on the Cape of Good Hope, a stopover on the trade route to Indonesia. Linnaeus gave it the name 'calla' in 1753, but it was changed several times because of confusion with other plants. More than a century later, the name *Zantedeschia* was proposed in 1826 to honour the Italian physician and botanist Francesco Zantedeschi

A calla lily in
the garden of Roslyn
and Robert Kaye,
Shushan, New York,
planted in memory of
their son James Kaye,
2011.

(1773–1846). It is a genus of the family Araceae that includes eight species with thick rhizomes and vase-like flowers wrapped around a prominent central spadix. The white *Z. aethiopica* was a popular flower in the nineteenth century and, as discussed in chapter Seven, became a psycho-sexual fad of early twentieth-century art and photography. It is the most familiar calla lily, although mini-hybrids in several other colours have been developed.

Water lilies are one of the most famous flowers in art, thanks to Claude Monet, who made them the subject of many paintings of the later years of his long career. These lilies are part of the family Nymphaeaceae, an appropriate name given its association with water nymphs in Greek mythology. Monet was intrigued not by mythology but by the play of water and light on his water lily pond, the highlight of his garden at Giverny. One of his gardeners did nothing else but care for the water lilies, removing dead flowers and dusting the carefully arranged lily pads every morning.[7] The artist did not limit himself to the common white and yellow indigenous species but instead chose exotically coloured hybrids, working closely with a grower who created them from Asian and African species.

The botanical sensation of the mid-nineteenth century was the giant water lily, *Victoria amazonica*, discovered in South America in 1837 and named in honour of Queen Victoria. Joseph Paxton coaxed it to flower in an English greenhouse in 1849 – a feat that earned him a knighthood – and the lily's fibrous leaf network of interconnecting ribs inspired him to design the cast-iron structure of the Crystal Palace in London, built in 1851. With their own unique DNA makeup, water lilies are not related to any other group of lilies. The first hybrid water lilies were tropical varieties bred in the 1850s to endure northern European winters. Today, the Nymphaeaceae family includes nearly 1,900 water-lily species and cultivars, a tantalizing selection for any artist's palette. While the lotus and the water lily are often

'Black Princess' water lily.

Claude Monet in his water lily garden, Giverny, around 1915–20.

Giant lily pads in the Helsinki Botanical Gardens, 2005. Discovered in the Amazon in 1837, this tropical plant is now grown in many parts of the world. Its leaf vein pattern was an inspiration for the iron-and-glass design of the Crystal Palace in 19th-century London.

grouped together, the sacred lotus of Asia belongs to a different botanical family, Nelumbonaceae. To make matters even more confusing, the blue lotus, *Nymphaea caerulea*, the sacred flower of ancient Egypt, is part of the true water lily family. Monet tried to include several species of lotus in his pond, but they failed to grow.[8] Most of the water lilies cultivated today originated in tropical regions, but the yellow pond lily or spatterdock is common throughout the northern hemisphere. Part of another Nymphaeaceae genus, *Nuphar*, it is found in Europe, western Asia and North America, where it was celebrated in Native American legends.

Close Relatives

Many other plants share the lily name. Some are botanical relatives of the true lily and others are just coincidental friends. Like many true lilies, three of its closest relatives are natives of eastern Asia. The giant lily of the Himalayas, *Cardiocrinum*, can reach as high as 13 feet (3.9 m) with white trumpet flowers as wide as 6 inches (15 cm). Standing tall at the back of perennial flower beds, it was the best lily for English gardens, according to Gertrude Jekyll (1843–1932), an influential British garden designer who had definite ideas of which plants were acceptable and which were not. *Nomocharis* are quite similar to true lilies except for their two distinguishing differences: fringed petals and blotched colours, reaching intense shades deep within the flower. *Notholirion* look something like miniature lilies, with many small, funnel-shaped flowers along a single stem. While most true lily bulbs live from season to season, these die after flowering, but produce tiny offspring, or bulbils, that produce the next generation.

Just Friends

Like a popular Facebook page, the true lily has lots of friends – plants that share its name but, like the water lily and calla lily, have little or no botanical connection to it. Although many of these vernacular

John Ruskin (1819–1900), *Field-lily of Oxford* (*Drosida ælfred*), before 1871, watercolour
sketch. Although Ruskin called it 'Alfred's Dew-flower', this member of the lily family
is better known as snake's-head fritillary (*fritillaria meleagris*) because of its chequered
petals that resemble the scales of a snake.

lilies have lily-like flowers, some look completely different from
the true lily, both above and below ground. Just to name a few, these
include the canna lily, lily of the Nile or African lily, also known as
agapanthus; the spider lily; trout lily; foxtail lily; peace lily; blood lily;
Kaffir lily; gloriosa or flame lily; lilyturf or plantain lily, also known as
hosta; and the belladonna lily or amaryllis, a native of South Africa. The

'Gloriosa', or flame lily, from a Mughal album of *c.* 1650.

last is an outdoor plant, not the common Christmas gift, also known as *Hippeastrum*, a South American import that blooms indoors from a large bulb. The belladonna, with flowers like a lily and leaves like a daffodil, was classified as a 'lilio-narcissus' in the early seventeenth century. The voodoo lily, a native of the Himalayan foothills, apparently gets its strange name from its eerie ability to grow and even flower without water, an adaptation to the dry Himalayan springtime.

Minoan 'Prince of Lilies', 1550–1540 BC, mural from the
Corridor of Processions, Knossos, Crete.

two

From the Ice Age to the Modern Age: *The Journey of the True Lily*

ᘒ

Cultivated and collected throughout the ages, the prolific genus *Lilium* may have the longest horticultural history of any flower blooming today. Its many species and hybrids in today's gardens have ancient roots in the Mediterranean, the Middle and Far East and North America. The family matriarch is the Madonna lily, *L. candidum*, whose origin, most likely in the Balkans, possibly pre-dates the Ice Age.[1] Its history of cultivation dates as far back as *c.* 1550 BC, the approximate date of its appearance on a wall painting in the palace of Minos at Knossos, uncovered in the early twentieth century on the Greek island of Crete. The flower's trumpet-shaped likeness was also discovered on Minoan pottery and jewellery, in ancient Egyptian tombs and on bas-reliefs from seventh-century BC Assyria (modern-day Iraq). 'Apart from trees, the Madonna Lily is the most identifiable plant in Assyrian art motifs', according to Penelope Hobhouse in *Plants in Garden History*.[2] The Greeks called it *krinon basilikon*, the royal lily. The Romans cultivated it, and Virgil gave it the name *candidum*, meaning shining or pure white. The name Madonna lily did not come into use until the nineteenth century, but it has links to Judaism as well as Christianity. It still grows wild in Israel, on Mt Carmel in Galilee, and some nursery listings compare its six pointed petals to the Star of David.

Lilies were part of ancient Rome's highly developed horticultural practices. Like other flowers, they were used for food, medicine, offerings to the gods and home decoration. Garlands of fresh flowers were draped on idols, thrown in the path of the caesars and heaped

Minoan pottery with lilies, 1400–1375 BC.

in their banquet halls. Fragrant lilies were especially desirable to perfume the air. Lilies were also painted on the walls of domestic buildings, as discovered in the ruins of homes in Pompeii and on the columns of their peristyle gardens. The Romans devised ways to grow lilies, as well as other flowers and vegetables, out of season in buildings heated by hot water. Amazing as it seems for its day, this technology was condemned by some Stoic philosophers. In his *Epistulae morales*, Seneca complained that 'men live contrary to Nature who crave roses in winter or seek to raise a spring flower like a lily by means of hot water heaters and artificial changes of temperature.'[3] The Romans spread *L. candidum* to all the countries of their empire. The legions planted it near their permanent camps to have the bulbs close at

Phoenician warrior holding a lily, 8th century, ancient Iraq,
ivory fragment possibly from a furniture inlay.

hand both for food and as a poultice, often mixed with animal fat, to cure corns.[4] Apparently, Roman sandals were not all that comfortable.

A great number of other species remained unknown to the West until intrepid travellers – sailors, pilgrims, missionaries, merchants and scholars – reached the New World and the East. While Europe descended into the Dark Ages, literally burying Rome's gardening innovations, horticulture and botanical scholarship continued to flourish in China, Japan and the Middle East. China is the homeland of nearly half of the 110 species of *Lilium* – more than any other country in the world.[5] As Jack Goody explains in *The Culture of Flowers*, Chinese horticulture, which had been 'more or less equal to that of the Greeks . . . for many centuries outshone the rest of the world'.[6] And while ancient Greek and Roman texts on botany were lost or beyond the reach of most people in medieval Europe outside monasteries, scholars in the Islamic world translated them into Arabic and made them available to eastern readers as early as the eighth century. By this time, Egypt, Assyria, Persia and Babylon were under Arab rule, and the Arabs had inherited the garden culture of those ancient civilizations. The Turks, originally from Central Asia, also had cultural contacts with China and India, and plants such as lilies from these countries also grew in the Ottoman Empire, which by the sixteenth century encompassed much of eastern Europe. When the Western world finally began to awaken from a long winter of ignorance, it was Muslim knowledge that led the way to a horticultural spring.

Western horticulture, like so many other fields of knowledge, began to revive during the Renaissance. With Gutenberg's invention of the printing press (*c.* 1439), books about plants and flowers began to reach beyond the cloistered worlds of medieval monks, and with the discovery of the New World, plants from the Americas began to reach Europe. One of the first North American lilies introduced to Europe was *L. canadense*, the Canada lily, sent by French settlers in about 1620. Tall with delicate bell-shaped flowers and whorled leaves, it grows wild in marshy meadows and thickets from Quebec to Alabama. Many other types arrived in northern Europe by way of trade with Spain and the Netherlands. Spain not only opened the door to European exploitation of the Americas but also had a rich horticultural heritage from the Moorish occupation.

The cultural wall between northern Europe and the Islamic world had a Berlin Wall-like moment in the sixteenth century. More than a hundred years after Constantinople fell to the Turks in 1453, the Holy Roman Empire, centred on Vienna, established diplomatic contacts with the Ottoman Empire. Ogier Ghiselin de Busbecq, the Holy Roman Emperor's ambassador to Constantinople from 1554 to 1562, was amazed by the flowers he saw growing in Turkish gardens and brought back bulbs that circulated around a network of European collectors. The rich variety of flowers from the eastern empire seems to give credence to a modern theory that Turkey was the site of the Garden of Eden. As the eminent British botanist William Stearn described:

> Never before or since has there been such an astonishing influx of colourful strange plants into European gardens, as when in the second half of the sixteenth century, importations of unpromising onion-like bulbs and knobbly tubers from Constantinople brought forth tulips, crown imperials, irises, hyacinths, anemones, turban ranunculi, narcissi and lilies.[7]

Tulips, of course, eventually became hugely popular, and in the 1630s led to the wild financial speculation and crash in the Netherlands known as tulipomania. But some of the most popular lilies also came from the Turkish Empire. The crown imperial, also known as the Turkish lily or *Fritillaria imperialis*, received its royal name from its association with the Holy Roman Emperor who opened the door to its arrival. Several species of true lily came to be called Turk's caps because their reflexed petals were thought to resemble turbans. They are also known as martagons. While martagons are also found in other parts of Europe, and in Asia and North America, one of the most popular, the scarlet Turk's cap, *L. chalcedonicum*, has a historic connection

Drawing with a red martagon lily border from *A Brief Relation of the Turckes . . .* (c. 1618). Also known as a Turk's cap, the martagon was thought to resemble the Turkish turban.

to Turkey. Named for the Chalcedon district opposite Constantinople, it was also known as the Byzantium lily, after the original name for the city. But it may have had an even earlier connection to Christianity. Some nineteenth-century Bible scholars believed that 'there can be little doubt that it is the plant alluded to by our Saviour' in the Sermon on the Mount. A far cry from the commonly perceived reference to a humble white lily, this showy red flower, they believed, might have been the one Jesus meant when he said 'even Solomon in all his glory was not arrayed like one of these'.[8]

The scarlet Turk's cap was an inspiration for many cultures. It also appears in the Islamic art of India of the early seventeenth century. In the 1630s Shah Jahan, the builder of the Taj Mahal, had exquisite miniature paintings of red martagons presented as gifts to his beloved wife.[9] They also appear on his cenotaph within that great building. Thousands of years earlier, the scarlet Turk's cap was a symbol of primitive religious observances. Archaeological discoveries in the twentieth century connected it to the religious rituals of the Minoan civilization in ancient Greece. An entire wall painting of these deep red lilies was unearthed in fragments on the Aegean island of Santorini, north of Crete. Nearly destroyed by an earthquake and volcanic eruption around 1500 BC – one of the largest eruptions in recorded history – the fresco was reassembled and is now on display in the National Museum in Athens. It is a unique portrayal showing lines of the red lilies, both in bud and bloom, growing on spectacularly shaped rocks.[10]

European traders had reached East Asia along the great silk roads of the Middle Ages, but plants did not often last the overland journey and, besides, spices were the goal of these arduous trips. Portuguese naval expeditions opened trade with China in the sixteenth century, followed by Dutch vessels that reached Taiwan in the seventeenth. Along with many treasures of the East, the Dutch East India Company brought back new plant specimens, generally as bulbs or seeds. Full grown, they inspired wealthy merchants and garden owners to commission flower paintings and illustrations that allowed the Dutch to marvel at the new wonders. Unlike most of their Catholic contemporaries in other countries, Dutch Protestant artists were painting flowers in nonreligious compositions and with almost scientific accuracy. The lush bouquet of flowers painted in *A Still-life of Flowers in a Wan-Li Vase* (1609–10) by Ambrosius Bosschaert the Elder displays many different types of flowers topped by a stem of white Madonna lilies. Most of the flowers in Bosschaert's painting are quite familiar today but, like the Chinese vase, they were considered exotic during this period of trade and discovery. The ubiquitous orange daylily, *Hemerocallis fulva*, which now grows like a native on New England country roads, was a Chinese import of sixteenth-century Europe. Nearly all the flowers proliferating today in Western gardens – including those as common as geraniums and petunias – were brought from other parts of the world between the sixteenth and nineteenth centuries. In 1500 there were perhaps 200 cultivated plants in England; by 1839 there were 18,000 – and the age of the great lily collectors had not even begun.[11]

Treasure Hunts in East Asia

European collectors did not open the treasure chest of lilies in East Asia fully until the nineteenth and early twentieth centuries. One of the first and most popular discoveries, the tiger lily, *L. lancifolium*, was sent from Canton (now Guangzhou) to Kew Gardens in London by William Kerr in 1804. A Turk's cap lily, it forms tiny black bulbils in each leaf axis, making it easy to propagate. The Chinese had a charming anthropomorphic description for its downward-facing form and reflexed petals – the 'Flower that turns its Head to See its Offspring'.[12] But the Japanese saw it quite differently. Its Japanese name is *oniyuri*, the ogre lily, and while its orange colour may account for the name tiger lily, its speckled petals seem more reminiscent of a leopard, albeit one with purple spots. (There is also a panther lily, *L. pardalinum*, a Turk's cap species found in California, but it also has spots.) A few orange-coloured lilies had made earlier appearances. *L. bulbiferum*, native to central Europe, is a remarkably realistic detail in the Portinari Altarpiece, of the Adoration of the Shepherds, commissioned by the Medici from the south Netherlandish painter Hugo van der Goes in 1475. It gets its name from the bulbils in its leaf axis, like those of the tiger lily. A variation, *L. bulbiferum* var. *croceum*, took on another sort of fame, or infamy, depending on one's political alliance. The chalice-shaped, tangerine-coloured lily became part of the Orangeman festivities held

Tiger lily with a butterfly, showing black bulbils at each leaf axis.

in celebration of the victory in 1691 of the Protestant William of Orange over the Irish Catholics who supported James II. Conveniently, the lily is in bloom at the time of the annual parades on 12 July in Northern Ireland.[13]

The spread of lilies followed British colonialism. In the mid-eighteenth century collectors sent many new flower species from the American colonies back home to Britain, including *L. superbum*. Commonly known from New Hampshire to Florida and Arkansas as a swamp lily, it was considered a superb specimen for its amazing height, up to 10 feet (3 m) and its profusion of martagon flowers, as many as 40 per stem. Despite its tropical-sounding name, the Bermuda lily, *L. longiflorum*, like so many other plants grown in the Caribbean, is not a West Indian native. Well known today as the Easter lily, it was discovered on the Ryukyu Islands of southern Japan by the Swedish plant explorer Carl Peter Thunberg (known as the 'Japanese Linnaeus') in 1776 and sent to Britain in 1819. British missionaries took it to Bermuda in 1853, and by the late 1880s it was in full commercial production there. The bulbs continued to travel, first to Philadelphia, then back to Japan, the west coast of the United States and from there to the global flower market. It all began with a Mrs Thomas Sargent, an American visitor to Bermuda who loved the flowers and brought back some bulbs to her Philadelphia home. She gave some to a local nurseryman, William Harris, who began forcing them into spring bloom and selling them to florists for the Easter holiday. In 1898 a virus destroyed the Bermuda crop and bulb production moved back to Japan, where it continued until the outbreak of the Second World War. After the war, large-scale production was developed by growers in California and Oregon, who marketed the white, trumpet-shaped species as the Easter lily. They currently produce 95 per cent of all the bulbs grown in the world for potted Easter lilies.[14] Readers of the Bible may be pleased to learn that Israel has also been producing variations of Easter lilies since the early 1990s.[15] The traditional

'Easter Lilies', illustration of Victorian shoppers in a flower shop, from *Harper's Weekly* (1892). Originally from Japan, the white trumpet-shaped lily was in full production in Bermuda by the 1880s and widely sold for Easter.

Easter lilies for sale on a Chicago street, 1941.

Easter lily used to be available only in white, but they are now produced in a variety of colours.

The Easter lily phenomenon was not the first peak of lily popularity in the West. The first ones to cause real excitement among everyday gardeners as well as collectors also came from Japan, a country that had restricted access to foreigners for centuries. The first successful collector to reach mainland Japan was the physician and scientist Philipp Franz von Siebold, who introduced many garden plants well known today, including new varieties of irises, hydrangeas, flowering cherries, plantain lilies (hosta) and true lilies. In 1830 he sent *L. speciosum*, a showy lily with wavy-edged petals still popular today, to Germany. It reached Britain two years later. The biggest celebrity of the nineteenth century arrived decades later, after Commodore Matthew Perry forced Japan to open its ports to international shipping in 1853. By this time, the invention of the Wardian case – a sealed portable greenhouse – made it possible to transport live plants, not just seeds and bulbs, on long voyages. In 1862 the British nurseryman John Veitch introduced what came to be known as the Queen of Lilies, *L. auratum*. As its Latin name implies, its petals have golden-yellow stripes.

It also has a delightful fragrance and the Chinese had cultivated it for centuries as *tian xiang*, or heavenly fragrance.[16] Its beauty — saucer-shaped flowers 12 inches (30 cm) across, dotted with crimson and striped with yellow — created a horticultural sensation in the West. Horticulturists raced to bring it to the British and American markets, introducing it at a Royal Horticultural Society show in London in 1862 and just ten days later at the Massachusetts Horticultural Society.[17] The result was near lily mania. The enthusiasm that greeted this spectacular flower is palpable in an English gardening guide written in 1879:

> Since the time when the Golden Banded Queen (Auratum), only a few years ago, burst upon us in her wondrous splendour — taking captive the startled senses of all, not merely horticulturists, but the public generally, by the enormous size and number of her flowers, their powerful fragrance, their elegant and graceful contour, their richness of ornamentation on a pure white ground, and by the general stateliness of the plant — the cultivation of Lilies has received a great impetus.
>
> Since that date, not only has Japan sent us Lily bulbs by tens of thousands, but America, both from her Eastern and Western Provinces, has contributed largely. India, Siberia, and the Caucasus, etc. etc., have furnished their quota, and Lily cultivators, who some ten or twelve years ago might almost have been counted on the fingers, are now to be numbered by the thousand.[18]

Victorians loved exotica. Already in the throes of *Japonisme* when *L. auratum* was introduced, they were in a frenzy to collect all things Japanese that were flowing into the West. Here was one more highly collectible thing of beauty — one that could reproduce itself each flowering season. The Victorian Orientalist painter John Frederick Lewis, who had established his reputation in the 1850s with watercolours full of the exoticism and mystery of Cairo and Istanbul, focused on Japan's prized Queen of Lilies. In 1871 he painted two women, a concubine and her attendant, dressed in Eastern costumes and gathering lilies in a harem garden. Despite the provocative subjects, the title of the painting is simply *Auratum*. Nearly a decade after the flower was introduced to the British public, its name was apparently still important enough to be used as the title. The women have hybrid facial features, suggesting that he used British rather than Japanese models. But there could be no mistaking the Queen of Lilies, which is depicted with careful accuracy.

The immense demand for this exotic and expensive flower, however, would prove nearly deadly. As Alice M. Coats reveals in *Flowers and their Histories*, the Queen of Lilies started a royal epidemic: 'the fat, soft, overfed bulbs . . . rapidly raised by the Japanese in response to the demand quickly fell victims to disease and gave the whole lily tribe a bad name.'[19] The family reputation was restored by the great British plant collector of the early twentieth century, Ernest Henry Wilson (1876–1930). An intrepid traveller who became known as 'Chinese' Wilson, he found China to be 'the Mother of gardens' and is credited with introducing approximately 2,000 plant species to the West, including one of the most famous garden lilies growing today. Starting out at the age of 23, he made six Asian expeditions for Veitch's nursery in England and Harvard University's Arnold Arboretum in Boston, Massachusetts. He struck gold on a trip in 1903 with the discovery of a new royal lily, the 'regal lily', *L. regale*. He found the trumpet-shaped beauty – each stem bearing ten or more flowers, white inside and purple outside – in the wilds of western Szechuan. His poetic description of the locale reveals his sense of ecstasy at the discovery:

Onward and westward up the mighty Yangtze River for 1,800 miles, then northward up its tributary the Min, in narrow, semi-arid valleys, down which thunder torrents, and encompassed by mountains composed of mud shales and granites, whose peaks are clothed with snow eternal, the Regal Lily has its home.

In summer the heat is terrific, in winter the cold is intense, and at all seasons these valleys are subject to sudden and violent wind storms against which neither man nor beast can make headway. There, in June, by the wayside, in rock crevices by the torrent's edge, and high up on the mountainside and precipice, this lily in full bloom greets the weary wayfarer. Not in twos and threes but in hundreds, in thousands, aye in tens of thousands . . . [20]

But the thrill of discovery soon met with disaster. Wilson's first collection of bulbs rotted in the hold of a ship and his return trip to the remote Min valley for more bulbs in 1910 nearly took his life. A rock avalanche crushed his leg, but he managed to set it using his camera tripod as a splint and was carried back to civilization, avoiding a highly risky amputation. The injury caused him to walk for the rest of his life with what he called his 'lily limp'. Despite the accident, he managed to send a shipment of bulbs back to the United States, where the lily was successfully introduced into cultivation. It is now considered one of the most important plant introductions of the twentieth century. Several other collectors explored China in the first half of the century, bringing back many other significant species. Frank Kingdon-Ward was on an adventure of his own when he discovered *L. mackliniae* in 1946. Working for the U.S. Air Force, he was searching for crashed American aircraft in Burma (now Myanmar) and happened to pick up an interesting-looking lily in seed. To his delight, it flowered two years later in Britain, producing unusual bell-like flowers.[21] Contemporary lily collectors have had their own adventures. B&D Lilies, a nursery in Washington state that catalogues native species, had an unusual experience while photographing the rare *L. occidentale* on the northern California–Oregon border, a haven for marijuana growers:

We were buzzed by a DEA [Drug Enforcement Agency] plane looking for pot growers until we stood up holding our now highly held aloft cameras. The pilot on his next pass gave us a wing wave and proceeded south continuing his patrol. Lesson learned? If you are going to grow pot in a dry bog in

Northern California, carry a camera bag large enough to be seen from the air.[22]

Taming the Wild Lily

By the Second World War, the heyday of the lily explorers was ending and the age of lily hybrids was just beginning. Although Chinese Wilson and others had introduced many new species from Asia, transplanting lilies from the wild had always been a risky procedure and everyday gardeners often found these expensive imports delicate and temperamental, requiring special conditions. For centuries, hybridizers had tried to combine different lily species to increase variety and improve their hardiness and resistance to disease. The science of flower hybridization had been established in the early eighteenth century when Thomas Fairchild (c. 1667–1729) transferred the pollen of a sweet William into the pistil of a carnation, creating the first documented artificial hybrid, known as 'Fairchild's mule'. Fairchild also developed a variety of the Madonna lily, *L. candidum* var. *purpurem*, with pale purple stripes on its white petals, although it no longer exists.[23] A more lasting lily hybrid, *L. testaceum*, reached Britain in about 1842. It was called the Nankeen lily, suggesting that it came from Nanking, China; however, it was said to come from a Japanese garden. The term 'nankeen' actually refers to its pale yellow colour, taken from a type of cloth made in Nanking. Experiments in 1895 revealed that it was actually a cross between the two ancient natives of Rome and Turkey, *L. candidum* and *L. chalcedonicum*.[24] Its origin remains a mystery; perhaps it was created by the hands of an unknown gardener or simply by birds, bees or wind.

During the first decades of the twentieth century a number of lily hybrids were successfully created by several breeders, notably David Griffiths, who introduced the Bellingham hybrids, named for his Washington state home town, in 1924. Several, including 'Shuksan' and 'Star of Oregon', are still popular today, but in Griffiths's day many hybrids were short-lived because of their susceptibility to disease. The horticultural establishment viewed them as little more than a flash in the pan. This all changed in 1941 when Jan de Graaff, a Dutch horticulturist who had moved to Oregon, succeeded in taming the wild lily. The talent was apparently in his blood. His great-grandfather, Cornelius de Graaff, had started hybridizing lilies in the Netherlands in 1790. Jan began his first lily experiments in 1938 at his Oregon Bulb Farms in Gresham, Oregon. Finally, in 1941, he produced 'Enchantment', essentially a tamed tiger lily, but one with a gorgeous hot coral colour, erect petals and a new hardiness. The gardening journal *Horticulture* called it 'the most famous hybrid lily of all time'. Still immensely popular in the garden and as a cut flower, it made De Graaff's fortune. Ever since, hybrid lilies have been the rule rather than the exception. After De Graaff's death in 1989, an article in *Horticulture* explained just what he had achieved: 'By dint of rigorous mass hybridization, de Graaff managed to ruin the lily's reputation as an impossible, unobliging garden aristocrat and made of the lily a good, easy-growing garden plant.'[25] De Graaff's success and that of the talented hybridizers who followed him led to a flood of lily production, particularly in lilies sold as cut flowers and potted plants. Commercial growers today raise them in greenhouses to provide a ready supply of brilliant lilies throughout the year.

Hybridization has produced an astonishing variety of lilies in nearly every colour, shape and size. More than 15,000 have been listed on the International Lily Register and just as many unregistered hybrids are believed to exist.[26] It is hard to keep track of all the hybrids making their debut in catalogues each year. Beginning in 1963, two standard-bearers of the lily world, the Royal Horticultural Society and the North American Lily Society, established an internationally accepted system of nine different divisions. Like the hybrids, the number of divisions kept increasing, but the eighth conveniently includes those not accounted for in any of the others. (The ninth includes species lilies.) The divisions are based on the species used to create the hybrids, distinctions that can be confusing to the average gardener. There are separate divisions, for example, called Asiatic and Oriental – a division that appears to be redundant. While both include crosses of species from

East Asia, each offers different advantages. Asiatics, largely the hybrids produced at the Oregon Bulb Farms and their descendants, are beautiful, virtually pest-free and amazingly hardy. Their only drawback is that, for the most part, they are also fragrance-free. Orientals, mainly derived from the two Japanese stars of the nineteenth century, *L. auratum* and *L. speciosum*, are very fragrant and flamboyant in size and colour. These two species had been crossed as early as 1869 by Francis Parkman, but the early Oriental hybrids were susceptible to the bane of lilies – virus disease. One of the most successful Oriental hybrids, the colourful and fragrant 'Stargazer', was finally created a century after Parkman's milestone. A cross between *L. henryi* and *L. speciosum rubrum*, it is a showstopping beauty with crimson petals edged in white and sprinkled with dark red spots. A breakthrough in lily breeding, it was created in 1978 in California by Leslie Woodriff, the father of the Oriental hybrid. Oriental lilies usually hang downwards, but Woodriff produced one with upward-facing flowers, hence its name, 'Stargazer'.

True lily species can be picky about their partners, but hybridizers have developed new techniques that, according to Arthur Evans, research director of the North American Lily Society, have allowed them to 'coax a miracle out of unlikely and unwilling pairs'.[27] The techniques, such as embryo culture, have created what might be called test-tube lily babies. The process involves placing seedpod embryos from distantly related species in a chemical solution. Judith Freeman, working at the Oregon Bulb Farms in the 1970s, produced one of the earliest successes, 'Tiger Babies', a pastel version of the orange tiger lily. Other new hybrids have crossed previously impenetrable borders between lilies in different horticultural divisions. Orientals and trumpets, for example, have been crossed to create Orienpets, a tall, big-flowered and highly fragrant hybrid. Some of the most popular Orienpets – 'Scheherazade', 'Starburst Sensation' and 'Regal Star' – have come a long way from the wild white lilies of ancient times.

But the current fashion for more natural gardens has also re-awakened interest in wild lilies. The latest trend in lily gardening is for 'purity gardens' of species lilies found only in the wild or propagated

'Stargazer' Oriental lily, grown by Maplecrest Lilies.

in their natural form by nurseries. As Robert Gibson of B&D Lilies wrote in 2008, the number of wild lily species being discovered is still growing:

> During the past few years, a number of 'new' lily species has been exported out of China from wild stands of bulbs, many still waiting to be properly classified. To think that every river or mountain side has been explored and there is nothing left to find is a mistake. Opportunities still await the plant adventurer.[28]

For all their myriad forms on the market today, hybrids have yet to take full advantage of the extraordinary diversity of wild lilies. Their amazing variations in colour, form, size, fragrance and other characteristics is 'seemingly endless'. If the untapped germplasm of the *Lilium* genus could be infused into the world of hybrids, the results would 'stagger the imagination'.[29]

The pond of water lilies at the Petit Palais, Paris.

three
A Lily in Every Garden

✤

From the Mediterranean cradle of civilization to the modern world, mankind has created pleasure gardens, and lilies have had a place in almost all of them. While speaking different languages and worshipping different gods, each civilization has sought places to escape the harsh elements and to experience a sense of repose surrounded by beauty. Even in the midst of arid deserts thousands of years ago, trees and flowers, including lilies, bloomed in enclosed and irrigated gardens. While fruit-bearing trees provided sustenance, space was also reserved for colourful flowers for pure enjoyment. Centuries after they were destroyed by warfare or simply deteriorated through age and neglect, the extensive gardens of the Roman Empire and the Italian Renaissance became green stage sets devoid of colourful scenery. But there is strong evidence that they were once filled with many different flowers, including the lilies native to the Mediterranean region. Lilies generally played a supporting role, but as more varieties were discovered and cultivated, their colours and scents added to the beauty of gardens and at times took centre stage. Their place in European gardens increased after the sixteenth century when exotic varieties from the Ottoman Empire began to reach the West. But they had been part of gardens for centuries before in their native lands of China, Japan, the ancient Mediterranean and Middle East.

The evolution of the art of botanical illustration and colour print-making techniques during the Renaissance ushered in the new science of botany, spreading information and appreciation for the intricate beauty of flowers. These developments went hand-in-hand with the creation of great gardens from the sixteenth century to the nine-teenth. Magnificent gardens were a luxury of the powerful and the wealthy, who often hired illustrators to record them in lavish folios. Over time, many more illustrations of gardens and flowers reached a wider audience – the rising middle class, who were eager to create their own beautiful gardens. This chapter will trace the thread of historic gardens that had the greatest influence on Western design, and the role of lilies within them.

Gardens in the Desert

Ever spreading, the desert has swallowed all but a few remnants of ancient Egypt's gardens. But discoveries inside tombs have revealed how the gardens must have looked. A doll's-house sized model of a garden was found in the tomb of Meketre, who was chancellor to King Mentuhotep II around 2000 BC.[1] Made of wood and painted green, it is a walled garden enclosing a pond and fig trees. The design is similar to gardens depicted in tomb paintings a millennium later. They show rectangular pools filled with water lilies, edged with flower beds and flanked with tall trees to provide essential shade from the blazing desert sun. The placement of pools comes as no surprise. The ancient Egyptians had to develop the science of irrigation in order to survive, and the pools and irrigation canals defined the recti-linear shape of their gardens. But the designs also reflected their spiritual life. The tomb paintings were symbolic representations of respite and refreshment for the soul's journey in the afterlife. They indicate the importance of the garden to the ancient Egyptians' sense of heaven. This is clear from a prayer inscribed on a tomb wall, asking that 'I may each day walk continuously on the banks of my water, that my soul may repose on the branches of the trees that I have planted, that I may refresh myself under the shade of my sycamore'.[2]

Tomb paintings can be seen as imitations of real gardens of the period. Tomb engravings and architectural motifs identify some of the flowers cultivated by the Egyptians and revered for religious significance, notably the sacred blue water lily, *Nymphaea caerulea*, and the trumpet-shaped Madonna lily. With other flowers, it is likely that these lilies were part of their actual gardens.

Roman Retreats

More than any other form of art, gardens are ephemeral, and most of the ancient ones have disappeared without trace. The unique exceptions are the structural remains of the gardens of Pompeii, preserved in volcanic ash after the massive eruption of Mount Vesuvius buried the entire town in AD 79. Since buildings also survived the catastrophe, it is clear that the walled gardens were located at the rear of homes and served as urban sanctuaries, open to the sky but protected from the noise and dust of the street. In *A History of Garden Design* (1963), Derek Clifford points out that these courtyard spaces were more rooms than gardens, because little sunlight could penetrate to support plants. Flowers were 'planted' with paint on the pillars of porticos and on the imaginative murals inside the houses. Surviving frescos depict idealized gardens filled with animals and identifiable flowers, including white lilies, no doubt the familiar Madonna lily of the Mediterranean.

The frescos provide the 'clearest picture of what the wealthy Roman of the time considered a garden should be'.[3] But Romans of great wealth were not limited to small urban retreats: they also had vast country villas encompassing extensive landscaped grounds and gardens. Much larger than modern estates, 'the Roman villa is difficult for the modern mind to compass', Clifford explains. 'It is said the estates of six men covered over half of Roman Africa.'[4] The emperor Hadrian's garden at Tivoli, created between AD 118 and 138, was a villa-city of multiple buildings, each linked by gardens. Only some of its foundations remain, discovered in excavations, and little or nothing is known about its plantings. Searching for lilies or any other single plant within these lost villas is like searching for a needle in the proverbial haystack. But the texts of ancient Roman authors provide some clues. Agricultural writers provided practical information for growing the plants used in imperial Rome. Varro's *De re rustica* (c. AD 40) is a practical farming manual with specific horticultural advice for growing flowers in great demand for garlands. Among many horticultural details, he notes the best time to grow lilies.[5]

Pliny the Younger provided a lasting description of the landscape of two of his Roman villas, near Rome and in Tuscany. Unlike his uncle, the naturalist Pliny the Elder, who died after inhaling volcanic fumes at Pompeii, the younger man lived to write about the eruption, which he had watched from a safe distance. He described his villas in letters written between AD 97 and 107. The Tuscan villa is the image of a classic Roman landscape. Centuries later, it would serve as the model for the gardens of the Italian Renaissance.

> The greater part of the house . . . is fronted by a broad and proportionately long colonnade in front of which is a terrace edged with box and shrubs cut into different shapes. From the terrace you descend by an easy slope to a lawn and on each side of the descent are figures of animals in box facing each other. You then come to a pleasance formed of soft acanthus. Here also there is a walk bordered by topiary work and further on there is an oval space set about with box hedges and dwarf trees.[6]

The estate extends through many other landscaped areas – open lawns, shady cypress groves, sunlit paths, small gardens, statuary and meadows. In the midst of this carefully orchestrated pleasure ground is a garden full of 'the careless beauties of nature'. Although Pliny does not name them, it is likely that the Madonna lily and other lilies native to the Mediterranean grew in his gardens and may well have been cultivated at other Roman villas as well.

Islamic Paradise

As Islam spread over the former Roman Empire in the seventh and eighth centuries, the Arabs enhanced the gardens of Rome. In Moorish Spain, their gardens became true paradises. Unlike the early Christian ascetics who saw Paradise only in Heaven, Muslims viewed gardens as a foretaste of Heaven for true believers. The predominant feature was water, the utmost luxury for desert dwellers. The Arabs built on the irrigation techniques developed by their predecessors in the Middle East – the ancient Egyptians, Persians and Assyrians – to create pools and fountains and to nourish fruit-bearing trees and fragrant flowers. Enclosed by protective walls, the gardens were divided into sections by the geometry of gravity-fed water channels that also symbolized the four rivers of Paradise cited in the Koran. The pools were filled with water lilies and lotuses, or simply reflected the sky, adding a greater sense of space within the high walls. The sound of moving water rippling over carved stone and bubbling in fountains added another sensual dimension to the colourful and scented surroundings.

Long before Europeans began collecting exotic plants, Arab botanists of the eleventh and twelfth centuries went on expeditions to Sicily, Alexandria, Cairo, Mecca and Valencia. They compiled long lists of the bulbs, herbs and flowers that filled the gardens of Arab and Turkish princes and hundreds of years later influenced garden design and plantings in India and the West.[7] The rose, closely associated with the prophet Muhammad, was the queen of flowers in Islamic gardens. But red lilies, inlaid in the floral patterns on the marble walls of the Taj Mahal and painted in Mughal miniatures of the same period, were always in close attendance.

During nearly eight centuries of Islamic rule in Spain, countless luxurious villas and gardens were established. All but a handful have disappeared without any surviving visual or written descriptions. The best preserved are the two famous gardens of Granada built during the last phase of Islamic control of the Iberian peninsula: the Alhambra, built in the fourteenth century, and the Generalife, built first on a

hillside above its current location in the mid-thirteenth century. These two, along with earlier Islamic gardens that no longer survive, had a lasting influence on gardens created by Christian rulers. Charlemagne, crowned Holy Roman Emperor in the year 800, may have seen Islamic gardens while on crusades in Moorish Spain. From his time onwards, Hobhouse maintains, 'it seems certain that attitudes to pleasure gardening were stimulated and enriched by Arab influences.'[8]

Gardens for Body and Soul

The ancient world's great traditions of pleasure gardening were lost to medieval Europe during the 300 years of chaos that followed the barbarian invasions of Rome. Apart from those created by the Moors in Spain, no actual garden made between the fall of Rome in the fifth century and 1500 exists today in Europe.[9] Latin texts on plants by ancient Roman naturalists such as Pliny the Elder were available only to medieval scholars, who were often cloistered in monasteries. The Venerable Bede (c. 673–735), the English monk who first described the Madonna lily as the emblem of the Virgin (see chapter Six), may have seen the actual flower growing in a monastery garden, since the Romans had spread it throughout most of Europe. But he also had access to a copy of Pliny's *Historia naturalis* of the first century AD.

Like most flowers grown in the medieval period, lilies were cultivated primarily for their medicinal value. Pliny's work and, most importantly, the first-century AD treatise on plants by the Greek physician Dioscorides, *De materia medica*, were copied and followed by herbalists until the nineteenth century. Herbs were the mainstay of medieval gardens, but manuscripts and art from the period suggest that flowers were also appreciated for their beauty and religious significance. Around 800 Charlemagne issued a decree, *Capitulare de villis*, listing the plants and fruit and nut trees that should be grown in each town to meet the need for food and for herbal medicine. The list is headed by lilies and roses, indicating not only their usefulness but

opposite: The water garden at the Alhambra, Andalusia, Spain.

also their Christian symbolism and beauty.[10] Like the Venerable Bede, other medieval monks equated their religious beliefs with a love of flowers. Alcuin of York (735–804), the founder of Charlemagne's palace school, the first university in northwestern Europe, spent the last years of his life as the abbot of St Martin at Tours, where he decorated his cell with white lilies and roses.[11] The German abbot Walahfrid Strabo, who created a garden in the ninth century on the island of Reichenau on Lake Constance in southern Germany, also extolled the virtues of the lily and the rose in terms of Christian symbols that would continue throughout history:

> Two flowers so well-loved and admired, that over the ages have stood as symbols of the greatest treasures of the Church, which has plucked the rose as a symbol of the spilt blood of the martyrs and which wears the lily as a shining symbol of faith; pluck the rose for war, the smiling lily for peace.[12]

By the eleventh century, scholars, pilgrims and merchants were travelling to Islamic Spain to study Arabic medical science. They very probably brought back new varieties of plants and bulbs, which eventually found their way into the gardens of the monasteries and palaces of Europe. In the fourteenth century Charles V of France had extensive royal gardens filled with flower and herb beds. Although they no longer exist, an inventory of the plants in his 20-acre garden at the Hôtel Saint-Pol in Paris survives. Among the many flowers listed are 300 lily bulbs.[13] Illustrations from books of hours, the richly decorated devotional books of the late Middle Ages, provide a visual record of the flowers grown during this period. Red and white lilies and lilies of the valley often appear in the margins of these books and in their illuminated scenes of heavenly gardens.

The Rebirth of Colour

'It may come as a surprise to many', Penelope Hobhouse explains, that the austere architectural gardens that survive from the Italian Renaissance today were once filled with 'colourful and exciting exotic flowers'. Created during a time when exotics were arriving in western Europe from the Ottoman Empire, Italian gardens were opulent with colour: 'Far from being flowerless, the gardens of the aristocracy, of the leaders of the church and of private botanists and collectors grew all the rare and exotic plants possible – including flowers.'[14]

Renaissance garden designers had little or no idea of the ruined gardens of Pompeii, which were not known until they were accidentally discovered in excavations for a new building project in 1748. But the surviving outlines of ancient villas in the hills of Rome and Tuscany served as models of symmetrical, terraced gardens for those able to emulate them. The writings of Pliny the Younger and other ancient authors rediscovered during the Renaissance fill in the empty spaces of these ruins with descriptions of trees, hedges and geometric flower beds.

In the second half of the sixteenth century the flower beds created for the magnificent gardens of the Medici and other princes of the Renaissance were settings for exotic arrivals from the East. Even before, according to Hobhouse, many exotics were already being grown in Italy, 'probably obtained through the Venetian Republic [and] . . . through far-flung contacts established by missionaries, especially Jesuits in the Far East'.[15] As Gill Saunders explains in *Picturing Plants*, while many plants were still grown in 'physic' gardens for medicinal purposes, by the early seventeenth century flowers were taking centre stage in purely decorative gardens.[16]

Horticultural treatises by Italian writers of the Renaissance provide descriptions of the plantings recommended for stately gardens. Writing at the end of the sixteenth century, Agostino del Riccio created an extensive list of trees and cultivated flowers, including twelve different kinds of lilies, for the imaginary garden of a king (*Del giardino di un re*, 1597). Since he disparaged growing wild flowers in formal beds, his recommendations were probably not limited to the area's prevalent Madonna lily. 'His extensive catalogue confirms the explosive arrival of "foreign" trees, shrubs, plants and bulbs which must have effectively revolutionized the appearance of gardens, at least those belonging to the aristocracy.' His contemporary Bartolomeo Taegio wrote *La villa* (1559), a tract on northern Italian country life, in which he recommends the scarlet Turk's cap lily, newly arrived from the Ottoman Empire.[17]

French Formality

According to Clifford, the French took the concept of the Italian garden and, 'after a very short time, made it their own'. The difference, to a great extent, was due to the lay of their land: 'French gardens continued to be on level ground or upon very slight inclines long after the Italians had taken to the hills.' Since terraces were not needed, the French 'particularly took to the parterre', or geometric planting beds. They continued the Roman and Italian Renaissance tradition of aligning the main house with the garden, but with formalized rules and intricate parterres. The French developed the 'notion of the garden seen as a horizontal one, for that essentially is the nature of a parterre; it is on the earth and to be looked down upon'.[18]

The classic French garden of the seventeenth century is best known in the expansive splendour of Versailles, with its intricate schemes of clipped trees in straight lines, sculpted box hedges, pools, borders and flower beds – all carefully placed for views from the palace. The geometry, laid out by André Le Nôtre, a master of garden design with architectural leanings, can be traced to the rectangular gardens of ancient Egypt and Islamic Spain. But the royal gardens of France were, above all, paragons of artifice. Each plant had its own space and was prevented from draping over the walls of the parterres.[19] And, to the greatest possible extent, each plant was a treasure. Although Le Nôtre cared more about the overall design than parterres of flowers,[20]

Louis XIV was an avid plant collector who sent explorers to many parts of the world to satisfy his continual demand for flowers in bloom. His collectors and growers developed vast collections of exotic plants and specialized in the newest arrivals of lilies, tulips and other bulbs from the southern and eastern Mediterranean, North Africa and the Americas. While other gardens of the European aristocracy also had encyclopedic collections of flowers and trees, the Sun King wanted his royal gardens to be growing and blooming at all times, even in winter. Versailles and the king's other royal gardens would be copied by the princes of Europe and by the Stuarts in England, particularly after the Restoration of Charles II in 1660, until the English created a revolution in garden design in the eighteenth century.[21]

The English Revolution

The English landscape parks of the eighteenth and nineteenth centuries created a revolution in garden design that swept away the French formality of geometrically organized garden beds. But it was a revolution that may have been based on a mistaken impression. When young eighteenth-century Englishmen on the European Grand Tour discovered the decaying gardens of the Italian Renaissance, they found them absent of all colour except the green and grey foliage of a terraced landscape. These gardens had once been radiant with colourful flowers, but they were now all gone, leaving a romantic scene of green pastoral beauty.[22]

The image reinforced the new romantic attitude towards nature that led to an appreciation for irregularity and a wilder look in gardens. The emphasis was now on a lush green monochrome of trees and shrubs uninterrupted by flower beds. Instead of conforming to the French style of tightly clipped branches, the English designers allowed trees to attain full growth in order to create a softer effect along undulating lawns and curving paths. The master hand shaping the new landscape was as influential in his day as Le Nôtre had been in France. Lancelot 'Capability' Brown (1716–1783) had little interest in rare or exotic species, but would 'move heaven and earth' to create a 'natural' effect. He widened rivers, created lakes, changed the contours of the land and planted tens of thousands of trees to create English land-scapes that looked as if nature alone had created them. The effect was naturalistic, but the plantings were not all native. Far-reaching scien-tific expeditions in the eighteenth and early nineteenth centuries were bringing back many different specimens from America and other outposts of the British Empire – South Africa, India, New Zealand, Tasmania and Australia; the port of the last was so famous for shipping plants that it was named 'Botany Bay'.

The English landscape style had a powerful influence on Ameri-can gardening. It led George Washington to introduce curving lines at Mount Vernon; inspired Thomas Jefferson's plantings at Monticello; and shaped Frederick Law Olmsted's plans for Central Park in New York.[23] The style still has a strong romantic appeal, sustained by British period films and television dramas. But at the same time, another, quite different image pulls the heartstrings of modern gardeners – that of the English cottage garden of colourful flowers. Flowers had their place in the landscaped park, artfully planted along curving walks to appear as if they had sprouted there themselves. Capability Brown's primary successor, Humphry Repton (1752–1818), was influential in bringing flowers back to the great English estates. They 'never really went out of fashion', Hobhouse maintains, but had been placed in beds and borders away from the principal views from the house.[24]

Giant Lilies Under Glass

While the lily was not the most popular flower of nineteenth-century British gardening, one very unusual lily played a large part in perfect-ing its greatest innovation, the greenhouse. In 1817 the Scottish botanist and landscape designer John Claudius Loudon invented the wrought-iron glazing bar and developed a hinged system for adjusting the angle of greenhouse panes to the angle of the sun. The development of sheet glass in 1833 and the removal of the glass tax in 1845 led to the manufacture of more affordable greenhouses.[25] The discovery of a giant water lily led to the greatest glasshouse of the century, the Crystal Palace. The giant Amazonian water lily was discovered in British Guiana by Robert Schomburgk in 1837 and became the most celebrated plant discovery of this era of great plant expeditions. Schomburgk named it *Victoria regia* in honour of Queen Victoria, but it was later renamed *Victoria amazonica*. In *Flora: An Illustrated History of the Garden Flower* (2001), Brent Elliott, librarian and archivist of the Royal Horticultural Society, describes the excitement that followed the discovery:

> It became a focus of media attention in England in the 1840s and the subject of three books. Gardeners from the Royal Botanic Gardens at Kew and the Duke of Devonshire's estate at Chatsworth raced to cultivate the first flowering specimen. Joseph Paxton, the Duke's celebrated gardener, won by building a special greenhouse for the plant (the prototype for the Crystal Palace).

Joseph Paxton (1803–1865) had the mind of a gardener and an engineer. He was impressed by the structure of the water lily's huge leaves, which one observer likened to 'some strange fabric of cast iron, just taken from the furnace'.[26] As a drawing of 1849 from the *Illustrated London News* shows, Paxton trusted one leaf to hold his daughter as she stood on it in the lily pool at Chatsworth. He had raised the plant from a seedling and described its amazingly rapid growth and large size:

> After receiving our young plant . . . on the third of August, 1849 . . . it must have added daily to its size the almost incredible number of six hundred and forty-seven square inches. This may be considered the most remarkable instance of the rapidity of vegetable development we have on record. Early in November, the leaves being four feet eight inches in

THE GIGANTIC WATER-LILY (VICTORIA REGIA), IN FLOWER AT CHATSWORTH.

'The Gigantic Waterlily (*Victoria Regia*) in Flower at Chatsworth', *Illustrated London News*, showing Joseph Paxton's daughter standing on a giant lily pad (1849).

diameter, and exhibiting every appearance of possessing great strength from the deep thick ribs, which form the foundation of the blade, I was desirous of ascertaining the weight which they would bear, and, accordingly, placed my youngest daughter, eight years of age, weighing forty-two pounds, upon one of the leaves; a copper lid, weighting fifteen pounds, being the readiest thing that presented itself, was placed upon it in order to equalize the pressure, making together fifty-seven pounds. This weight the leaf bore extremely well, as did several others upon which the experiment was tried.[27]

The following spring at Chatsworth, the water lily produced 24 huge leaves, some reaching more than 5 feet (1.5 m) in diameter, which were able to support adults: 'we have had both ladies and gentlemen, from eight to eleven stone weight [approximately 112 to 154 lbs] trying the experiment, and the great buoyant power which they so evidently possess gives the individuals thus standing on them a feeling of perfect safety'.[28]

Knighted for his gardening achievement in 1850, Paxton went on to design the Crystal Palace, using the intricate rib structure of *Victoria amazonica*'s leaves as the model for the iron structure supporting the plate glass – the largest amount of glass ever seen in one building. It opened in Hyde Park in London in 1851 to display the latest wonders of the Industrial Revolution. Rebuilt in 1854 in the London suburb of Sydenham, it became an important showcase for exotic plants, inspiring more greenhouses and more beds of colourful flowers in British gardens. Greenhouses became the foundation for the Victorian fashion for massed flower beds. The new species arriving from tropical locales were protected from cold weather in greenhouses, where they thrived in potted British soil. With the arrival of spring, these tender annuals – scarlet geraniums, purple petunias, blue lobelias and many others – were set out in beds, each one massed with a single bright colour and changed periodically to ensure a continuous display of blooming flowers. The practice was taken up by the new middle classes, who took their cues from greenhouse flower shows in public gardens and the flood of books and journals produced for the gardening public.

Back to the Wild

True lilies and other hardy flowers were overshadowed for a time by the showy displays of annual blooms. But by the late nineteenth century the hardier flowers had gained new champions. William Robinson (1838–1935), a crusader against hothouse-grown flowers, started a new revolution in British gardening, a reactionary one that rebelled against the current reign of artificial practices and advocated a more natural garden. In *The Wild Garden* (1870) and *The English Garden* (1883), as well as countless journal articles, he attacked the brightly coloured beds of 'foreign' flowers as 'the ugliest gardens ever made' and pushed instead for hardy beds of perennials like those in old-fashioned cottage gardens. His views were much like those of the artists and other proponents of the Arts and Crafts Movement, who reacted against the machine age of the Industrial Revolution in favour of more natural, handmade products.

Robinson's best-known disciple, Gertrude Jekyll (1843–1932), who designed some 400 gardens in Europe and the United States, developed the art of perennial flower gardening into a widely influential style that is still popular today. She softened the garish colour contrasts of Victorian beds with a painterly approach that used graduated hues and textures in drifts of billowing flowers. Foreign perennials, even lilies from East Asia, were acceptable if they 'behaved like natives'. In one of her many books, *Lilies for English Gardens: A Guide for the Amateur* (1903), she recommended the lilies that would naturalize in British soil, and no doubt influenced the creation of the famous gardens of her friend Vita Sackville-West at Sissinghurst Castle in Kent. While Japanese gardens became a brief fad in the 1890s as part of the *Japonisme* era of decorative arts, the Robinson–Jekyll approach for more natural gardens prevailed throughout the twentieth century. Its influence can also be seen in today's ecological gardens of native plants and 'purity' gardens of wild species lilies.

Sissinghurst Castle gardens, Kent, England.

Star of the Show

Commercial growers, of course, still rely on greenhouses to produce colourful annuals each spring. At the same time, botanical gardens have turned the increasing number of hybrid flowers into displays on a massive scale. The largest lily exhibition ever mounted in North America took place in May 2010 at Longwood Gardens in Pennsylvania, one of the nation's largest botanical gardens. Called 'Lilytopia', the show included 10,000 lily stems and 210 cultivars of hybrid lilies, many new to the market.[29] Longwood, which covers more than 1,000 acres of indoor and outdoor gardens, is a descendant of the great gardens of Europe. It was founded in the early nineteenth century by the industrialist Pierre du Pont (1870–1954), who was inspired by his visits to the Crystal Palace in Sydenham (which stood until 1936) and the Royal Botanic Gardens at Kew, as well as the grand gardens of Italian villas and French chateaux. Billed as the 'New Golden Age of Hybrid Lilies', 'Lilytopia' displayed the flowers in 3.7-m-tall (12-foot) columns, arches and a 'wall of lilies' containing 1,000 stems. The show was produced in conjunction with members of the Dutch bulb industry, which includes some of the world's largest lily growers. The 'biggest lily show in the world' took place in May 2011 at Keukenhof garden in Lisse in the Netherlands, home of the annual Lily Parade.[30]

One hundred and sixty years after Paxton's feat, horticulturists at Kew Gardens marked another milestone in raising water lilies, this one noted for its miniscule size. The world's smallest water lily, *Nymphaea thermarum*, just a centimetre wide, had vanished from the wild but was saved from extinction in 2010. Discovered along the muddy edges of a hot spring in Rwanda in 1985, its only known location, it had died out after the water that fed the spring was diverted to agricultural use. With just a few seeds remaining and after much trial and error, the Kew horticulturist Carlos Magdalena succeeded in propagating the tiny species.

overleaf: Kew Gardens horticulturist Carlos Magdalena holds the world's smallest water lily next to the giant water lily. Just a centimetre wide, the tiny lily had vanished from the African wild but its seeds were discovered and propagated at Kew in 2010.

In the future, the ultimate achievement in lily gardening may come as the result of global warming. Like Paxton using the giant water lily as a model for the Crystal Palace, the visionary Belgian architect Vincent Callebaut created 'Lily Pad City', a model for a floating city that looks like a mega-sized lily pad. Designed in 2008, the self-contained structure would include housing, marinas, plants to filter waste water for reuse and other innovative facilities to sustain 50,000 climate refugees from low-lying coastal lands inundated by rising sea levels.

'Lily Pad City'. Vincent Callebaut's architectural model for a floating city, based on the structure of lily pads and designed in response to rising sea levels.

Life cycle of a moth on a lily by Maria Sibylla Merian, *c.* 1691–9. Merian was one of the first women to achieve recognition as a botanical artist.

four
Picturing the Lily

৵Ɛ

look at two botanical illustrations of the Madonna lily, one from the Middle Ages and the other from the late Renaissance, reveals the radically different attitudes of these two eras towards science and the natural world. The medieval illustration has a history much longer than its own. It was discovered in a German herbal of the early thirteenth century, but was copied from a sixth-century manuscript that was possibly copied from the first-century work of Dioscorides. This illustration of the Madonna lily is a stylized portrayal of three stems in flower, complete with the bulb. In contrast, the Renaissance illustration, portrayed by Pieter van Kouwenhoorn, a Dutch illustrator, around 1630, is a precise and richly coloured drawing of the lily at the height of flowering, focused on every detail of the white blooms. It reveals the artist's keen observation of nature and almost sensual delight in the beauty of the flower. The difference between the two illustrations is more than a technical tale of the evolution of printing. It also explains the dawn of the new science of botany and man's empirical reawakening to the beauty and diversity of the world.

More than any other science, botany depends on pictures. The fragility of plants and even dried specimens, which lose their living colour and form, make scientific study difficult. Botanical illustrations made plants visible and reproducible for analysis. They evolved from hand-drawn copies and crude woodcuts of stylized plants in medieval herbals to finely detailed copper etchings and splendid

An Arabic illustration of the late 10th century based on a drawing from *De materia medica*, created in the first century by the Greek physician Dioscorides.

colour lithographs in lavish folios, books and magazines. In the process, which unfolded over centuries along with new botanical discoveries and developments in printmaking techniques, they presented a more complete natural history of nearly every plant and flower, including extraordinary images of many different kinds of lilies.

The famous treatises of the ancient Greeks and Romans were followed for millennia, but without clear visual reproductions they often became confusing at best and, at worst, hopelessly inaccurate. The original manuscripts of Pliny and Dioscorides 'were lost and have survived only as copies of copies', Gill Saunders, a curator of prints and drawings at the Victoria and Albert Museum, London, explains in *Picturing*

Plants.[1] For practical and cultural reasons, the woodcut method of reproduction was unreliable. Used repeatedly, woodblocks often blurred the lines of drawings, making their subjects barely identifiable. Although Dioscorides said he produced his treatise 'with very accurate diligence, knowing most herbs with mine own eyes',[2] medieval herbalists continued to rely on poorly copied manuscripts as unshakable authorities, as well as on myth, folklore and superstition, rather than on direct observation. Clouding nature even more, woodblocks were often altered in the style of the day to include decorative flourishes such as curlicues or to add a leaf or a branch for the sake of symmetry.

A thirteenth-century drawing of the Madonna lily looks more like folk art than realistic representation, but it is one of the few botanical illustrations of its period that is readily identifiable. Western artists perhaps focused more attention on its likeness because of the flower's importance as a Christian symbol. As naturalism slowly emerged in fourteenth-century Italian art, the Madonna lily seemed to lead the way. Giotto 'still made trees like outsize herbs', says Wilfrid Blunt in *The Illustrated Herbal*, 'and for much of the trecento almost the only recognizable flower in the paintings of Tuscan artists was the occasional Madonna lily'.[3]

But it was earth-shaking events, not religion, that led to the highly developed naturalism of botanical illustration in the Renaissance. The development of improved printing techniques made it possible to reproduce illustrations with precise clarity and to reach a much wider audience. Expeditions into new lands opened the eyes of the medieval world to first-hand observation. Instead of copying old texts, illustrators were called on to document newly discovered species. Artists accompanied voyages of exploration just for this purpose, to capture the appearance of a mature plant in flower before it died or changed irreversibly on the long trip home. In the midst of great gardens, they worked hand in hand with the growing number of botanists. Medieval herbals, like their ancient predecessors, were concerned almost exclusively with the medicinal value of plants. But by the seventeenth century botany was emerging as an independent science apart from

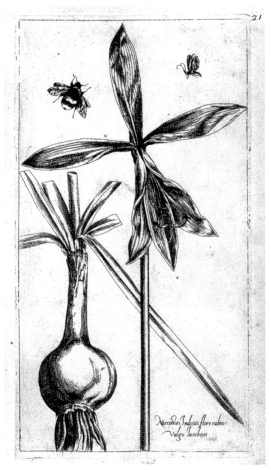

21

A Jacobean lily (*Sprekelia formosissima*), from Pierre Vallet, *Le Jardin du Roy très chrestien, Loys XIII* (1623). Native to Mexico and also known as the Aztec lily, this bulbous plant may have been brought to Europe by early Spanish explorers.

medicine, and its focus was shifting to images of plants and flowers for their own sake. It was the beginning of an age of great botanical activity, of people devoting their lives to the new science and to the acquisitive thrill of possessing exotic treasures.

Like many of the great gardens of the age, the art of botanical illustration developed in the European centres of trade and colonial power. New specimens from far-off lands arrived in the ports of Germany, the Netherlands, France and Britain, and were sold to collectors for botanical study and private gardens. Woodcut printing had been vastly improved by two German illustrators, Hans Weiditz and Leonhart

Fuchs, who in the sixteenth century created 'living portraits of plants' based on their own observations. (Fuchs's name was commemorated in the fuchsia plant, discovered in the Caribbean in the late seventeenth century, and it is also the origin of the name for the plant's purple-red colour.) Weiditz created the illustrations for one of the most famous herbals of the time, the *Herbarum vivae eicones*, first published by the botanist Otto Brunfels in 1530. Brunfels wanted to stick to the medicinal plants cited by Dioscorides, but Weiditz drew nature as he saw it, including full-page drawings of water lilies.[4]

By the early seventeenth century flowers were increasingly grown, not only for food or medicine but also purely for their beauty and decorative qualities. To preserve and catalogue the splendour of their gardens, the wealthy and powerful commissioned artists to create illustrated folios known as florilegia. The first significant one, *Hortus Eystettensis*, was published in Nuremberg in 1613 as a record of the garden of the bishop of Eichstatt. Created by an apothecary, Basil Besler, it was not limited to medicinal plants but documented more than 667 of the exotic specimens the bishop had collected from all over the world, including a vibrant illustration of the orange *L. bulbiferum*. According to Nancy Keeler in *Gardens in Perpetual Bloom*, it 'marks the transition from the period of woodcut-illustrated herbals to large folio volumes illustrated with copperplate engravings' and 'became the standard for later florilegia'.[5] On 28 November 2001 a copy sold at Christie's in London for $1.4 million, the highest price yet paid for a botanical book.[6] Florilegia focused exclusively on cultivated flowers, not wild flowers. Some specialized in lilies and other new bulbs arriving from the East, such as tulips, daffodils and other narcissi. They were also used as pattern books for flower painting on porcelain and in other decorative arts. Herbals and florilegia would later influence Arts and Crafts artists such as William Morris in creating patterns of lilies and other flowers for textiles, rugs and wallpaper.

The greatest botanical illustrator of the mid-eighteenth century, Georg Dionysius Ehret (1708–1770), created a record of the Amsterdam garden of George Clifford, a British banker based in the

Netherlands. In 1737, working closely with the Swedish botanist Linnaeus, he produced *Hortus Cliffortianus*, the first work to illustrate dissections of flowers. His illustrations helped to promote Linnaeus' revolutionary theories of plant classification and new botanical terminology, published the same year as *Systema naturae*. Linnaeus' theory of classification (later replaced by a more sophisticated system) was based on the sexual parts of plants. He recounted that Ehret was reluctant at first to paint these reproductive details:

> Ehret did in the beginning absolutely not want to paint the stamina, pistilla, and other small parts, as he argued they would spoil the drawing; in the end he gave in, however, and then he liked this kind of work so much that thereafter he observed the most minute and inessential particulars.[7]

Ehret's later illustration of the American lily, *L. superbum*, reveals his delight in detailing the flower's prominent pistils, stamens and anthers meticulously while at the same time creating a drawing of great beauty. Unlike earlier illustrations in herbals, his drawing of the lily shows no roots, bulbs or seeds. His focus, like other illustrators of this period, was on the flower itself. Ehret was part of a vibrant centre of botanical activity in Europe. He painted the American lily in the London garden of Peter Collinson, a cloth merchant who dabbled in botany and distributed plants from North America. Collinson received the first *L. superbum* bulb in 1736 from Philadelphia farmer John Bartram, who sent thousands of plants, bulbs and seeds from the colonies to Europe.[8] The painting was included in *Plantae selectae* (1750–65), a folio published by the German physician Christoph Jacob Trew, a collector of botanical illustrations, including the seventeenth-century originals from *Hortus Eystettensis*.

In 1786 the French illustrator Pierre-Joseph Redouté (1759–1840) adopted a new colour printing technique that made him the most celebrated illustrator of his day. The technique, stipple engraving, in which masses of dots are applied to the areas of the printing plate

Tab. XI

LILIVM *folus sparsis,*   *multiflorum, floribus reflexis,*
fundo aureo, limbo auran-   *tio, punctis nigricantibus,*
    pedunculis singulis   *unico folio instructis.*

Christoph Jacob Trew (1695–1769), *Lilium foliis*, hand-coloured engraving after George
Dionysius Ehret. Known as the American swamp lily, this tall, multi-flowering species
was later given the more attractive name *L. superbum*.

receiving coloured ink, enabled him to reproduce the delicate nuances of flowers. Employed by the Empress Josephine in 1802, he worked for the next fourteen years to create *Les Liliacées*, 508 sumptuous plates of lilies, daylilies and other flowers in her extensive plant collection at Malmaison. The title is a little misleading since many of the flowers in the book, such as orchids, are not in the lily family. Redouté also included the plantain lily, or hosta. Introduced from China to Britain in 1790, it was still relatively new to cultivation and classified as a blue daylily. Today it is grouped in the Asparagacea family.

A hugely ambitious and idiosyncratic collection of botanical illustrations was launched at the end of the nineteenth century by Robert Thornton, a British physician and professor of medical botany. Nothing compares with his *Temple of Flora*, and to many critics that may be a good thing. Intended to outdo every other work of botanical art, it began as an ardent effort to 'trace the philosophical principles of botany from the earliest times up to the present period' and was presented in three volumes. The third, the *Temple of Flora*, was to include 70 large, lavishly coloured illustrations of exotic plants displayed against supposedly appropriate, but often overly theatrical, backgrounds. 'The Superb Lily' (*L. superbum*) is set against the wild-looking mountains that Thornton must have imagined in eastern America. The 'Blue Egyptian Water-lily' is set on the Nile along with an explanation that mixes botany with the author's patriotic zeal. Written during the Napoleonic Wars, just a year after Nelson's victory of 1798 against the French at the Battle of the Nile, a good part of the text is devoted to the battle, along with a gloating list of the destroyed French ships. Thornton wrote the text but hired the leading botanical artists and engravers of the day to create the illustrations. The work proved highly expensive and although it had many wealthy subscribers, including Queen Charlotte and other members of British and foreign royalty, it met with mocking reviews and led to Thornton's financial ruin. Only 31 of the illustrations were completed, and it became a white elephant. But the work still carries a legendary reputation. Over the years it has been reissued as individual prints and in book form. The most recent,

Striped white lily (*L.candidum* var. *purpureum*), watercolour by Jacobus van Huysum, 1723–46.

PLATE VII.

1 *Lilium lancifolium album*   2 *Lilium lancifolium roseum*

Lilium lancifolium and L. *lancifolium roseum*, hand-coloured etching, illustration to Robert Thompson's *The Gardener's Assistant* (1859), one of the many horticultural periodicals that flourished in the nineteenth century.

issued in 2008, was a full-size facsimile, larger than most coffee tables and weighing nearly 30 lb (13.6 kg).

Botanical art reached its peak production in the nineteenth century. As Alice M. Coats explains,

> More illustrated flower books were published in the first half
> of the nineteenth century than in the whole of the eighteenth,
> and almost twice as many as in the sixteenth and seventeenth
> together. Both black-and-white and colour reproduction reached
> a standard that has never since been surpassed, largely owing
> to the skills developed by artists, engravers and printers, in
> response to the demands of botanists.[9]

As gardening became increasingly popular, botanical illustrations found new outlets in periodicals that combined botanical discoveries with horticultural information. Published in Britain, France, Belgium, Germany and America, they appealed to a wide readership. Many of the plants discovered in the nineteenth and twentieth centuries had their debut in *Curtis's Botanical Magazine*, first published in London in 1797 by William Curtis, an apothecary-turned-botanist, and still produced by the Royal Botanic Gardens at Kew. Veitch Nurseries, one of the most important plant collectors in the nineteenth century, displayed more than 400 of its plant introductions in the magazine, including the wild lilies discovered in Asia by Ernest 'Chinese' Wilson. An illustration of the white calla lily, *Zantedeschia aethiopica*, in 1805 by the magazine's first illustrator, Sydenham Teast Edwards, is as lush as a twentieth-century painting by Georgia O'Keeffe. After Edwards left to start a rival magazine, the prolific illustrator Walter Hood Fitch (1817–1892) took over and produced some 2,700 drawings for the periodical. Fitch, who began his career as a fabric designer in Glasgow, created a total of 10,000 botanical illustrations for various publications. Among his most famous are the illustrations of lilies for *A Monograph of the Genus Lilium* written by the plantsman Henry John Elwes (1846–1922), who collected many species in the Himalayas. The monograph, compiled of lavish plates produced from 1877 to 1880, was 'one of the culminating ornaments of the Victorian Age', according to Sacheverell Sitwell in *Great Flower Books, 1700–1900* (1956).

Fitch also created beautiful hand-coloured illustrations of the giant water lily, *Victoria regia* (now *amazonica*), published in 1851 in a separate volume in celebration of Paxton's success of 1849 in getting the plant to flower. They were part of a series of ground-breaking achievements in botanical illustration focused on this amazing lily. The plant had become a phenomenon even before Paxton's accomplishment, a testimony to the passionate public attention given to botanical discoveries in the nineteenth century. Shortly after its discovery, the British botanist John Lindley published a folio monograph of the giant water lily. After Paxton's flowering feat, several others also succeeded, including two Americans, both amateur botanists: Caleb Cope near Philadelphia in 1851 and John Fisk Allen in Salem, Massachusetts, in 1853. Just as they had done in England at Paxton's greenhouse at Chatsworth, crowds of people came to see the giant lily in bloom in America. 'I am sorry you were not here to witness the excitement which prevailed when the Victoria bloomed for the first time in this country', Cope wrote to a friend, 'my grounds seemed to be in complete possession of the public.'[10] Cope's head gardener described the continuing excitement and amazement in a letter to the editor of the popular American periodical *The Horticulturist* in 1852:

> The interest which characterized the flowering of the Victoria in this country continues unabated . . . It would not be extravagant to call the beauties of this plant unsurpassable. Like the gigantic idea its leaf-structure originated – the Crystal Palace – it stands among its class alone and unapproachable.[11]

William Sharp, an artist and lithographer, was commissioned to illustrate the lily at Allen's greenhouse. He created six plates of the prodigious leaves and spectacular flowers in successive stages of growth. Nancy Keeler calls his use of colour lithography, known as chromolithography,

Henri Baillon, lily of the valley botanical print, 1885–95.

H. BAILLON.   Iconographie de la Flore française.

CONVALLARIA MAJALIS L. — *MUGUET DE MAI.*

'the foundation of colour printing in America'. As she describes, his illustrations were as ground-breaking as getting the plant to flower:

In a sequence resembling a time exposure, Sharp made drawings of the flower as it began to open and at subsequent stages right up to full blown. The leaves, which approached six feet in diameter, were considered as important as the flower. With a rim that stood up three to five inches, coloured green on the inside and red on the underside, they were like fantastic, floating salvers. Sharp drew the underside, showing the extraordinary thick ribs

91

of the architecture that supported the vast surface expanse. His drawings were made with specific understanding of the painstaking chromolithographic process, an awareness that perhaps accounts for the subtle tonal renditions he achieved.[12]

Sharp's plates, together with Allen's detailed text, were published in 1854. While it also described Paxton's achievement, the title of the book, *The Great Water Lily of America*, gives America top billing for this South American discovery and British horticultural first.

While men had achieved prominence as botanical artists over several centuries, women were comparatively rare in the profession before the nineteenth century. But they had always been active participants in the field. In the mid-seventeenth century Maria Sibylla Merian (1647–1717) combined the detailed artistry of the Golden Age of Dutch painting with scientific precision. Born in Germany to a family of engravers, she travelled to Surinam and was one of the first Europeans to record the plant and animal life of the tropics. But Merian's individual achievements were the exception. Teams of women worked unnoticed in botanical book production, colouring the black-and-white illustrations by hand. The wives and daughters of nurserymen also became skilled in the field in order to help the family business by illustrating catalogues of their flowers. In the eighteenth century drawing and painting flowers was considered a pastime only for well-bred women. Its popularity was led by British royalty, notably George III's wife, Queen Charlotte, who also studied botany. A number of botanical books, including Thornton's *Temple of Flora*, were dedicated to the queen. (Four new varieties of apple were also named in her honour, as well as the dish 'apple Charlotte'.)

Despite printing innovations in the first half of the twentieth century, *Curtis's Botanical Magazine* used only hand-coloured plates before 1948.[13] Yet their female employees were not all behind the scenes. After Fitch's resignation in 1878, Matilda Smith became the chief artist. Lilian Snelling was the magazine's chief artist from 1922 to 1952, and among her individual accomplishments was the supplement to Elwes's *Monograph on the Genus Lilium* in the years 1934–40. The pre-eminent botanical

A Madonna lily (*L. candidum*) from Maria Sibylla Merian, *Histoire des insectes de l'Europe . . .*
(1730).

artist of the late Victorian era was Marianne North (1830–1890), who
travelled the world, largely alone, painting unusual vegetation and
flowers. Her gallery, the first by a female botanical artist, opened at
Kew Gardens in 1882. North's detailed oil paintings of plants never
seen before in Britain were all the more remarkable in the age
before photography.

Considering the Lilies before they Burn

Partners for centuries, the art of botanical illustration and the science of botany parted for a time with the invention of modern photography. Many botanical and horticultural publications abandoned nuanced illustrations. Yet a new wave of appreciation for botanical art and its enduring role in scientific illustration emerged in the late twentieth century. One of the major reasons for its renewed popularity was the recognized need to document species endangered by global warming and expanding development in wilderness areas. Many of the species Merian and North painted in the tropics have since disappeared. In the mid-twentieth century another extraordinary artist and intrepid traveller, Margaret Mee (1909–1988), documented the disappearing plant life of the tropics and sounded an early alarm about its exploitation. More fearless than the artists who accompanied voyages of exploration in previous centuries, Mee, a petite middle-aged woman, made solo journeys into the Amazon rainforest, at times accompanied only by native guides. Reaching remote areas in a dugout canoe, she sketched exotic species, including the night-flowering water lily *Nymphaea rudgeana*, and brought them back to Rio de Janeiro to be cultivated. Four previously unknown species were named after her. In the twenty-first century, botanical artists continue to accompany scientific expeditions to document new discoveries. The American artist Susan Coffey was part of the team led by the plant morphologist Donald S. Byrne to find a rumoured new dwarf species of the Victoria water lily in Brazil in 2007. They discovered it on the banks of a tributary of the Amazon. She had just three days to draw every detail of the plant, which became an invaluable record when it was submitted to the International Lily Register and formally presented to the Brazilian government.[14] Leading botanists today, such as Sir Peter Crane, former director of Kew Gardens, believe that botanical illustration is 'as important today as it was three hundred years ago'. 'The skills that can capture the essence of a plant, document its structure, and at the same time create a work of great beauty, are still in demand. They have not been displaced; not even by the most sophisticated of modern cameras.'[15]

Refocusing on Flowers

Embraced by major institutions, an increasing number of talented artists have created a renaissance in botanical art. The Hunt Institute for Botanical Documentation, founded in 1961 as a research centre and library at Carnegie Mellon University in Pittsburgh, includes an expanding collection of work from Georg Ehret to Margaret Mee and Anne Ophelia Todd Dowden (1907–2007), known as 'America's leading botanical artist'. In 2000 the Brooklyn Botanic Garden established its own florilegium society, a term rarely used since the seventeenth century, to 'reinvigorate that centuries-old form of botanical illustration'. Composed of 'some of the country's most accomplished botanical artists', the group is documenting the garden's living collections of flowering plants, including its famous pools of water lilies. In 2008 Kew Gardens, long the premier centre for botanical scholarship and art, opened the Shirley Sherwood Gallery of Botanical Art to exhibit both historical and contemporary work. A great variety of botanical art is being produced today, in the form of scientific documentation, book illustrations and imaginative works of sheer beauty, sometimes with an unusual subtext. Commissioned by a financial institution, the contemporary artist Lisa Holley painted daylilies in an arrangement that loosely outlines the Dow Jones chart for the decade from 1980 to 1990. One dead flower represents the 'Blue Monday' crash of 1987.[16] Like the species they illustrate, botanical works of art have become collectible items themselves. Modern colour printing techniques have made them accessible to a wider public still eager for visions of botanical beauty.

Jacopo Tintoretto, *The Origin of the Milky Way*, depicting Hera with Heracles at her breast, *c.* 1575, oil on canvas. It was said that milk spurting skyward from her breast created the stars, and the drops that fell to earth became white lilies. The lilies originally at the bottom of the painting can no longer be seen because the lower part of the canvas was torn off when the painting was plundered in the 17th century.

five
Milk, Blood and Sex:
The Mythology of the Lily

❦

W hether goddesses or saints, mothers are formidable figures in ancient religions. Their sexuality may be flaunted or forbidden, graphic or mystical, yet underlying its many manifestations is a reverence for fertility, a quality often symbolized in pagan and Christian legends by the lily.

Mothers are passionate creatures in Greek and Roman mythology. In the legend of Hera, mother of the gods and goddess of women and marriage, lilies were created from the essential nurturing element, mother's milk. Myths, of course, are not botanically specific, but the colour of milk is a strong hint that this was the white *L. candidum*, well known to the Greeks and Romans. The story is one of clashing wills, deception and unmotherly behaviour. Known as Juno by the Romans, Hera was the wife – and also the sister – of Zeus or Jupiter, god of the sky and father of all gods and man. Zeus, who fathered offspring by many other women, wanted one of his illegitimate children, Heracles (Hercules), the son of a mortal woman, to become an infant god. He asked Hera to nurse the child so that her milk would make him immortal. Hera, a jealous and vengeful wife – during his mother's labour she had tried to prevent Heracles from being born – refused adamantly. Zeus gave Hera a sleeping potion and placed the child at her breast. He sucked so hungrily that Hera awoke and pushed him away, splashing milk across the heavens and in so doing, forming the Milky Way. The drops that fell to earth became white lilies.

This ancient myth was cited in the first century BC by Gaius Julius Hyginus, a Latin scholar and librarian to Caesar Augustus. It found its way into a Byzantine botanical textbook, *Geoponica*, the probable source for Tintoretto's great painting *The Origin of the Milky Way*. His powerful portrayal of the myth presents the gods as muscular figures hovering in the heavens, and stars shooting out from Hera's breasts. But it does not show the lilies – and this is a story in itself. The painting, with the lilies on the ground, was acquired by Emperor Rudolf II, who fancied himself as a version of Heracles and 'liked to have himself portrayed wearing a lion's skin and carrying a club'.[1] Tintoretto had painted the lilies at the bottom of the painting but, nearly a century later, this part of the original canvas was lost in the midst of an invasion at the end of the Thirty Years War. In 1648 Swedish soldiers looted the painting from the imperial palace in Prague and in the process lost one-third of the canvas.[2] It now hangs, minus the lilies, in the National Gallery in London. The myth nonetheless pops up in many other places, such as John Gerard's *Herball*, first published in 1597 in England. Gerard calls the white lily 'Juno's Rose because as it is reported, it came up of her milke that fell upon the ground'.

The personification of the anti-mother is Lilith, Adam's first wife, a figure derived from Jewish folklore. Her name may have evolved from that of the Etruscan goddess of death, Lenith, who met the dead at the entrance to the underworld. In some versions of the story, the entrance was in the shape of a lily. In various legends of other ancient cultures, she is a demon of the night who kills or kidnaps newborn children and sleeps with men to seduce them in orer to conceive demon sons. Fear of Lilith continued for centuries. A fearsome illustration of around 1930 by Henry Keen portrays her as a scowling nude. The ground at her feet is littered with skulls and lilies, their stigmas like erect phalluses.

The sexual implications of the lily are more subdued in other ancient legends. The goddess Ostara of Norse mythology is the spiritual protector of young love and marital bliss. While she heralds the

Henry Keen, *Lilith, c.* 1925–30, lithograph. The lilies growing at the feet of this legendary demonic figure are depicted as sexually sinister plants.

coming of spring, the season of fertility, she is a virgin goddess. Some historians see her as a pagan predecessor of the Virgin Mary. The spring-blooming lilies of the valley are linked to both figures as symbols of renewal, and also in Christianity as a sign of the Resurrection. The lily was also associated with Ishtar of the ancient Near East, another virgin goddess of fertility. Linguists, including Jacob Grimm, the author of the famous fairy tales as well as *Deutsche Mythologie* (1835), traced the etymological evolution of the names Ishtar and Ostara to Easter.

White lilies have been linked with the Virgin Mary as early as the second century. In Christian tradition from this period, Mary's tomb, visited three days after her death, was found empty save for roses and lilies. These two flowers, traditional symbols in Latin poetry – red roses representing passion and white lilies, purity – passed into Christian iconography, where red roses stand for Christ's blood and white lilies for Mary's purity. Mary was not only a virgin mother, according to Catholic doctrine, but was also free from original sin from the moment of her conception. Not accepted at first, the doctrine of the immaculate conception was rejected by the Dominicans, but with Franciscan support gained increasing popularity in the fifteenth century. Carlo Crivelli's painting *The Immaculate Conception* (1492), which includes a stem of white lilies in a clear glass vase as a symbol of the Virgin's purity, may be the earliest dated picture illustrating this doctrine. It was formally proclaimed as a dogma by Pope Pius IX in 1854.

Christian and Native American legends merged in the figure of Kateri Tekakwitha, known as the 'Lily of the Mohawks', a seventeenth-century Christian convert in upstate New York. She was beatified in 1980, the first Native American to be canonized by the Catholic Church. Her shrine, located near Schenectady, New York, is a National Park Service Historic Site. Born in 1656, the daughter of a Mohawk chief, she was only four years old when her parents and brother died of smallpox. She survived the disease but it left her face badly scarred and her eyesight impaired. Converted to Catholicism by French missionaries, Tekakwitha took a vow of chastity at the age of eighteen and led a legendary life of goodness, unwavering faith and dedication to the Virgin Mother. She died in 1680, shortly before her 24th birthday. Witnesses claimed that 'within a few minutes of her death, the pock marks from smallpox completely vanished and her face shone with radiant loveliness.' Others testified that she appeared to many people after her death and was responsible for healing miracles.[3]

While the image of Mary as an exalted virgin mother has been fixed in Christian tradition throughout the ages, it has been transformed through the lens of some contemporary historians. In *Re-imagining Mary: A Journey through Art to the Feminine Self* (2009), the Jungian analyst Mariann Burke argues that the Christian concept of a virgin birth is based on pagan legends of self-fertilization. More to the point, she sees the lily as the embodiment of this theory: 'The lily in mythology and classical symbolism represents the Goddesses' power of self-fertilization. The Roman Goddess Juno used her lily in this way when she conceived the god Mars, for all hero gods were born miraculously.'[4] Burke is referring to a tale by the Roman poet Ovid in which even the passionate Juno (Hera) gives birth through a virginal conception, although in this case it is inspired by Juno's jealousy. Jealous of Jupiter (Zeus), who had given birth to Minerva (Athena) directly from his forehead, Juno asked Flora, the goddess of flowers, how to conceive a child on her own. Flora gave her a magical lily and, simply by touching it, Juno became pregnant with Mars. For this reason, Mars was revered by the Romans not only as the god of war but also as the guardian of agriculture.

In ancient Greek and Roman wedding ceremonies, the brides wore crowns of lilies as a sign of fertility. Some Greek and Roman myths specifically involve the physical characteristics of the lily, graphically describing the pronounced male and female features of the species and suggesting self-fertilization. Aphrodite (Venus to the Romans), the goddess of love, beauty and sexual passion, is often represented with a rose. Jealous of the beauty of lilies, she 'gave them a pistil reminiscent of the phallus', according to Marina Heilmeyer in *The Language of Flowers*.[5] The act was a perverse distortion, since the pistil, which contains the plant's ovary at its base, is the female part of the flower and is surrounded by the male stamens bearing pollen. Ironically, true lilies are actually self-sterile. They will not produce seeds if their own pollen is placed on their own stigma, the tip of the pistil. In other words, cross-fertilization has to take place between two different plants. An ironic footnote to the Aphrodite myth is that the modern lily cultivar named 'Aphrodite' has been bred to have no pollen. Nursery advertisements boast that it can be placed in flower arrangements 'without the fear of messy pollen stains'. Perhaps the cultivar's name is a sly reference to the goddess's mythological birth, the result not of sexual intercourse but of her father's castration. His severed member was thrown into the sea, giving rise to his daughter's emergence from a seashell, famously painted as the *Birth of Venus* by Botticelli.

The rose has battled the lily throughout the history of literature for the title of Queen of the Flowers. Shakespeare alludes to it in *Henry VIII* when Queen Katherine finally agrees to step down as the king's wife: 'Like the lily that once was mistress of the field and flourish'd, I'll hang my head and perish' (III, i, 151–3). A light-hearted allegory of the feuding flowers unfolds in William Cowper's poem 'The Lily and Rose' (1782). The goddess Flora steps in to resolve the conflict with fairness to each flower. At the end of the tale, Cowper combines the colours of the two flowers in a tribute to British beauty:

> The nymph must lose her female friend,
>   If more admired than she –
> But where will fierce contention end
>   If flow'rs can disagree?

> Within the garden's peaceful scene
>   Appear'd two lovely foes,
> Aspiring to the rank of queen –
>   The Lily and the Rose.

The Rose soon redden'd into rage,
 And, swelling with disdain,
Appeal'd to many a poet's page
 To prove her right to reign.

The Lily's height bespoke command –
 A fair imperial flow'r
She seem'd designed for Flora's hand,
 The scepter of her pow'r.

The civil bick'ring and debate
 The goddess chanc'd to hear,
And flew to save, ere yet too late,
 The pride of the parterre.

Yours is, she said, the nobler hue,
 And yours the statelier mien,
And till a third surpasses you,
 Let each be deem'd a queen.

Thus, sooth'd and reconcil'd, each seeks
 The fairest British fair;
The seat of empire is her cheeks,
 They reign united there.

The romantic metaphor of lilies and roses in a woman's fair complexion was a familiar conceit of the eighteenth and nineteenth centuries. Even the scientific-minded Linnaeus used it in naming the *Amaryllis belladonna* (beautiful lady) because of its pink-and-white flowers.

Lily Lore

Several types of lilies are the subjects of other far-ranging legends, at times erotic, violent, poignant or heroic. Heracles reappears as an adult in the myth of the water lily, the beginning of a story entwined with the lily and the lotus. A water nymph, Lotis, is enthralled by Heracles' virility but he does not return her enamoured gaze and she dies heart-broken. Hebe, the goddess of youth and spring, turns Lotis into a water lily with purple flowers. Her sister nymph, Dryope, later comes upon the water lily, but when she picks it, the stem drips blood. Dryope is turned into a lotus shrub, bearing the fruit of forgetfulness that seduces the lotus-eaters in the Homeric legend.

In Ovid's poetry, water lilies are flowers of sinister seduction. Heracles, now Hercules in this Roman version, together with his young page Hylas, is sailing with Jason and the Argonauts in search of the Golden Fleece. When they stop on the island of Cios, Hylas goes in search of a pond to quench his thirst. He approaches one filled with water nymphs. They urge him to join them in the water and, when he refuses, drag him below the surface. Hercules, hearing Hylas' cries, searches for the boy but never finds him – and the *Argos* sails off without them.

The story is sensuously realized in a painting, *Hylas and the Nymphs* (1896), by John William Waterhouse. In *Flora Symbolica: Flowers in Pre-Raphaelite Art*, the art historian Debra Mancoff gives a vivid description of the painter's sexual depiction of the tale:

> The nymphs . . . appear to be water lilies in human form. With their alabaster skin, tinged with the slightest blush of arousal, and their streaming auburn hair, they emerge from the water's depths in a random circle, floating like the lilies on the opaque surface of the pond. In Christian tradition, the water lily represented unsullied purity, but in the later nineteenth century, the stagnant water that nurtured the blossoms gave the symbol a sinister dimension. Like sirens and mermaids,

who entranced men to make them their captives and victims, the water nymphs embodied the male horror of female sexuality; their innocent beauty disguised their insatiable desire to plunge hapless men into their foul domain.[6]

The Native American myth of the origin of the yellow water lily has a similar narrative, although one in which the roles are reversed. In this case it is the young man who causes the supernatural figure to perish in the water. The Star-Maiden from the night sky visits a Dakota chief and tells him that she wants to come to earth to live with his tribe. The chief tells his son to take the maiden in his canoe to reach the tribe's wise man who lives across the lake. Paddling quickly in the darkness, the boy hits a log and the Star-Maiden falls into the water and disappears. 'The next morning, growing at the spot where the maiden's light was extinguished was a water lily with yellow flowers gleaming in the sun.'[7]

In an early Christian legend, lilies of the valley emerge after a fierce battle between the hermit St Leonard and the Devil disguised as a dragon. Although Leonard was a sixth-century saint from France,

John William Waterhouse, *Hylas and the Nymphs*, 1896, oil on canvas. In Ovid's ancient tale the nymphs, depicted here as water lilies in human form, lured Hylas to a watery death.

the legend is linked to St Leonard's Forest in Sussex, England, where a section of the woods is still called the Lily Beds.[8] The story tells of days of fighting, at the end of which St Leonard finally cuts off the dragon's head, but not before the beast's claws have pierced the saint's armour. Charles Montgomery Skinner (1852–1907), an American writer who published collections of myths and legends, gives a romantic account of the age-old tale:

> Wherever its claws or tusks had struck him and his blood had dewed the earth, heaven marked the spot and sanctified it, for there sprang the lily of the valley. Pilgrims might trace his encounters in white all about the wood; and those who listened could hear the lily bells of snow chiming a round to victory.[9]

Skinner relates two other medieval folk tales that use lilies as parables, the first concerning fleeting happiness, the second unquestioning Christian faith. In the first, a knight in old Normandy falls in love with a lovely woman sitting on a tombstone and holding a lily. She agrees to become his 'lily wife' on one condition: that he never speak of death. 'Think of me as representing the life of the world, the bloom of youth, the tenderness of love, and think of this as yours forever', she tells him. After many happy years together, the knight inadvertently sings a song that mentions death, and his wife 'faded like a flower touched with frost'. He clasps her in his arms but she turns into a lily, its petals dropping on to the floor.

In the other tale, a young boy, an 'innocent or imbecile', is taken into a monastery in Seville. The brothers try to instruct him, but he can do only menial tasks. He would 'steal into the church and sit alone murmuring, "I believe in God; I hope for God; I love God"'. One day he is found dead, but with a smile on his face. After his burial, a lily springs up from his grave. The abbot orders his body exhumed, 'whereupon it was found that the heart of the innocent had become the root of the flower'. The story is similar to a folkloric belief that lilies,

Sophie Anderson, *Elaine*, 1870, oil on canvas. In Arthurian legend, Elaine died of a broken heart and is seen here clutching a white lily as a sign of her innocence.

unplanted by human hand, appear on the graves of innocents executed for crimes they did not commit.[10]

Lilies are also important symbols in the Arthurian legends as interpreted by nineteenth-century poets and artists, who were entranced by medieval mythology. Alfred Tennyson's *Idylls of the King* (1856–85), twelve poems narrating the tales of King Arthur and the Knights of the Round Table, inspired many painters of the era. In 'Lancelot and Elaine', Tennyson made the lily the symbol of the innocent young Elaine, the Lily Maid of Astolat, who died of a broken heart because of her unrequited love for Lancelot. Her tragic death is portrayed poignantly in Sophie Anderson's painting *Elaine*, in which the young maiden is carried on a funeral barge, clutching a lily in her cold, white hand. In the poem, Arthur had her buried in a tomb engraved with a lily as a sign of her chaste girlhood cut short and as a caution to those who would corrupt the innocent.[11] The idyll of the Holy Grail, the story of the knights' spiritual quest for the cup from which Jesus and his disciples drank at the Last Supper, is illustrated in a magnificent series of six tapestries by

Edward Burne-Jones, 'The Attainment', from the *Quest for the Holy Grail* tapestries, 1896, Panel 6: 'The Vision of the Holy Grail to Sir Galahad, Sir Bors and Sir Percival'. Galahad stands next to tall lilies, signifying his pure character.

the Pre-Raphaelite painter Edward Burne-Jones. In the final scene, 'The Attainment', completed in 1896, the three successful knights, Bors, Perceval and Galahad, are shown outside the chapel in which the Grail stands on an altar surrounded by angels. Galahad, who had the purest heart, is closest to the chapel. He kneels in the door-way, flanked by tall stands of white lilies symbolizing his purity.

A dramatically different picture of the lily appears in the mystical mythology envisioned by William Blake (1757–1827). As part of his complex philosophy, the poet rejected the sinfulness of sexual acts and instead portrayed sex as essential to the merger of body and spirit. In the illustration he drew for his epic poem *Jerusalem: The Emanation of the Giant Albion* (1804–21), a nude couple embrace within the petals of a giant lily.

The Italian legend of St Paulinus (*c.* 354–431) is celebrated today in unique lily festivals held from Naples to New York. In Italy, it is called the Festa dei Gigli, Italian for lily, and in Brooklyn, the site of one of the largest *gigli* festivals in the United States, it is known as the Giglio. The legend tells of Paolini, also known as St Paulinus, bishop of Nola, a small sea port south of Naples. Around the year 400 the town was invaded by North Africans, who enslaved the men and boys. According to the legend, a widow, whose only son was taken, appealed to the bishop for help and he offered himself in exchange for the child. After several years as a slave, he won his freedom and

William Blake, illustration from *The Song of Los* (1795).

that of the men of Nola. As they returned home, the women of
the town greeted them waving lilies. Festivals in Paulinus's honour
grew from simple presentations of lilies to the church in the town
centre to parades with lilies and a statue of the saint mounted on

Every ornament of perfection. and every labour of love,
In all. the Garden of Eden. & in all the golden mountains
Was become an envied horror. and a remembrance of jealousy:
And every Act a Crime. and Albion the punisher & judge.

And Albion spoke from his secret seat and said.

All these ornaments are crimes. they are made by the labours
Of loves: of unnatural consanguinities and friendships
Horrid to think of. when enquired deeply into; and all
These hills & valleys are accursed witnesses of Sin
I therefore. condense them into solid rocks. stedfast.
A foundation. and certainty and demonstrative truth:
That Man be separate from Man, & here I plant my seat.

Cold snows drifted around him: ice coverd his loins around
He sat by Tyburns brook. and underneath his heel. shot up!
A deadly Tree. he namd it Moral Virtue. and the Law
Of God who dwells in Chaos hidden from the human sight.

The Tree spread over him its cold shadows. (Albion groand)
They bent down. they felt the earth and again enrooting
Shot into many a Tree! an endless labyrinth of woe!

From willing sacrifice of Self. to sacrifice of (miscalld) Enemies
For Atonement: Albion began to erect twelve Altars.
Of rough unhewn rocks. before the Potters Furnace
He namd them Justice, and Truth. And Albions Sons
Must have become the first Victims. being the first transgressors
But they fled to. the mountains to seek ransom: building A Strong
Fortification against the Divine Humanity and Mercy
In Shame & Jealousy to annihilate Jerusalem.

William Blake, illustration from *Jerusalem: The Emanation of the Giant Albion* (1804–21).
Lilies were part of Blake's mystical imagery.

Lily festival in Nola, Italy. The towers in this drawing of 1868 are covered with lilies in celebration of the 5th-century story of St Paulinus's return from slavery.

poles. Throughout the Middle Ages and the Renaissance, artisan guilds vied with one another to design the tallest towers representing the lilies and carried them through the town. The tradition continues in Nola today with teams of men carrying eight huge spires. In the late nineteenth century immigrants from Nola began to settle in Williamsburg, Brooklyn, bringing the festival with them and passing its tradition on to generations of Italian Americans. Starting in 1887, the annual event has now become a joyous spectacle centred around an 80-foot-high (24 m) *giglio* tower made by the local residents and painted with lilies. Topped with a statue of Paolini and decked with loudspeakers and an Italian flag, it is mounted on a platform that also carries a twelve-piece brass band and singer. The entire assemblage, both tower and band, is lifted and carried by 130 dancing and marching men. They march through the streets in a series of lifts, carrying the 4-ton load for about 9m (30 feet) at a time. Each lift begins with the festival song, 'O

Giglio e Paradiso'. Written in 1959, the song rises to a crescendo with each lift, inspiring the men and the crowds to bounce along the route, 'dancing the Giglio'. In more recent years the band has added popular music, including the theme song from the movie *Rocky* (1976).

L'ange de la pureté (The Angel of Purity), French print, 1878.

six

As Pure as a Lily

U nlike the ancient myths that revel in conflict and sexuality, Christian art portrays the lily solely as a symbol of purity and chastity. But this icon, so fixed in Christian art, took centuries to take root. Flowers in Christian services, as in the Eastern religions of Buddhism and Hinduism, seem always to have gone together – yet this was not always the case for Christianity. In *The Culture of Flowers* (1993), the social anthropologist Jack Goody makes a strong case that flowers were anathema to early Christian beliefs. Under Roman rule, Christians were eager to distinguish their religious practices from those followed by the Romans. Draping statues of the gods with garlands of flowers was seen, by Jews as well as Christians, as pagan idolatry. Rome's highly developed floral culture died out after the barbarian invasions and was replaced to a great degree by Christian asceticism. It rejected flowers, both on religious and moral grounds, as the trappings of hedonism and sin.

To Christian ascetics, paradise was to be found in Heaven, not in earthly gardens. While the Old Testament does not specify particular flowers in the Garden of Eden, the phrase from the Song of Songs, 'a lily among thorns', eventually became a metaphor for Christ and his Virgin Mother. But the prominence of flowers in Roman culture led some early Christian writers to warn that flowers were sinful, even wanton. Lactantius, a fourth-century Christian convert, condemned the presence of prostitutes at the Roman festival of Floralia and charged that the goddess of flowers was herself a harlot.[1] The story was revived by seventeenth-century Puritans in England and New England as justification for their objections to the rites of May. To the Puritan mind, the practice of gathering lilies of the valley, a flower once called 'ladder to heaven', was a sinful act. Even herbs, the basis of medicine from ancient times until the Renaissance, were suspect as tools of witchcraft by some early Christians, who advised saying prayers while picking useful flowers.[2]

Over the course of several centuries after the fall of Rome, Europe regained the lost culture of flowers and Christians began to adopt them as religious symbols. The writings of the English monk the Venerable Bede cited the lily as the emblem of the Virgin Mother's purity, 'the pure white petals signifying her spotless body and the golden anthers her soul glowing with heavenly light'.[3] By the twelfth century flowers had returned to royal and monastic gardens in Europe, to popular usage and to poetry. By this time, the French monarchy had adopted the fleur-de-lis as its heraldic emblem, with its implication of divine authority.

Fleur-de-lis: Lily or Iris?

Like the biblical references to the lily, the history of the fleur-de-lis is a tale of myriad meanings. Closely linked with Christian iconography in the Middle Ages, it nonetheless pre-dates Christianity and can be found on ancient artefacts and coins from Mesopotamia to Indonesia. In ancient Crete, Egypt, India and Rome, the design was often found on elaborate jewellery and as the head of a sceptre, indicating that it was a royal insignia. Some historians see it as a trident or arrowhead, but most agree that it is a stylized flower – one that resembles an iris, specifically *Iris pseudacorus*, the yellow flag iris common in many parts of Europe. Although *fleur-de-lis* is French for 'lily flower', the name itself is the subject of debate. One theory traces its etymology to the French king Louis VII (1120–1180), who is said to have adopted it as his sovereign emblem, known then, in Old French, as *flor de Loys*, or 'flower of Louis'. Centuries later, it was known as 'flower-de-luce', a term Shakespeare used in *The Winter's Tale*. Yet he included it at the end of a long list of flowers as a type of lily (IV, iv, 126–7):

> The crown imperial; lilies of all kinds,
> The flower-de-luce being one!

While the golden fleur-de-lis of the French monarchy may look like an iris, in Shakespeare's day and even in the much earlier time of Louis VII, who was known as one of the most pious French kings, it was clearly linked to the lily's established meaning as a symbol of Christian purity. In the mid-fourteenth century the French used it as a convenient argument for the monarchy's divinely sanctioned authority, a response to the challenge to the French throne by Edward III of

'Clovis recevant la fleur de lys', from the Bedford Book of Hours (1423). In the legendary Christian conversion of the first French king, Clovis I, angels delivered the fleur-de-lis, establishing the flower as the symbol of the Bourbon monarchy.

England at the start of the Hundred Years War. The argument reached back to the Christian conversion of the first French king, Clovis I, in 493, citing a legend that angels carried a banner to Clovis bearing three fleurs-de-lis. Signifying the Holy Trinity, they replaced the original three crescents on his coat of arms, signs of his Muslim origins. The event is beautifully illustrated in the Bedford Book of Hours of 1423. Other versions of the legend make an even stronger case against Clovis' 'pagan' origins by maintaining that his original arms did not feature crescents but toads.

Octave Guillonnet (1872–1967), *La Marche sur Reims*, watercolour. A depiction of Joan of Arc accompanying Charles VII to be crowned at Reims. The banner emblazoned with fleurs-de-lis signifies the re-establishment of the Bourbon monarchy after Joan of Arc's victories over challengers to the French throne.

Frans Pourbus the Younger (1569–1622), oil painting of Marie de' Medici wearing an elaborate gown of fleurs-de-lis after she became Queen of France in 1610.

Joan of Arc carried a banner imprinted with fleurs-de-lis into battle and, after her victory in 1429, her family was given the noble title Du Lys. Although she lost the title when she was condemned as a heretic and burned at the stake, images of her as a saint still bear the symbol. French kings kept the fleur-de-lis as a sign of their divine sovereignty, emblazoning it on their royal robes in official portraits. Despite her Italian origins, Marie de' Medici (1573–1642), who became queen of France after the death of her husband, Henry IV, in 1610, is a formidable figure in her coronation portrait, wearing a tent-like gown and robes covered with fleurs-de-lis. By the early nineteenth century the identification of the fleur-de-lis with the lily was clearly linked to the Bourbon monarchs, who traced their sovereignty back to Clovis I. With the Bourbon Restoration, after Napoleon was forced off the throne in 1814, an allegorical engraving entitled *France Makes Lilies Blossom Again* shows a figure, clothed in a robe decorated with fleurs-de-lis, watering a stand of white lilies. The fleur-de-lis has also been the emblem of the city of Florence since medieval times, although in somewhat different form. Known as the Florentine lily, it has lily-like stamens between the petals.

Lilies also became part of church services during the Middle Ages, draped over altars and incorporated as symbols in the liturgy. Jungian psychologists see the reappearance as part of a continuous flow of archetypal symbols from the pagan to the Christian era – for example, the adoption of the rose and the lily from ancient myths to classical Latin poetry to icons of the Virgin Mary – but it also had its practical benefits. Priests found flowers, even wild flowers, to be useful tools in teaching the faith to their largely illiterate parishioners. Goody explains that 'Just as gardens were "christianised" by being brought into the monastery, flowers were baptised with "Christian names".'[4] Many of the most common European wild flowers were renamed so as to associate them with the Virgin. Canterbury bells, or foxgloves, for example, became 'Our Lady's gloves'. During the Reformation in the sixteenth century, many of these names were stripped of what were considered to be 'popish' associations, but many still persist in common usage today without the prefix 'Our', such as 'lady's mantle' for *Alchemilla*.

Early medieval paintings of the Garden of Eden were often stark. As Derek Clifford describes in *A History of Garden Design*, 'more often than not the garden of Eden is represented as a small circle of ground surrounded by a paling fence and containing two trees, one snake, and two disconsolate human beings who would appear to have had little to lose.'[5] But by the thirteenth century visual representations of the Garden of Eden in medieval European art began to bloom with flowers. And in the art of the Renaissance, the lily came to its full flowering as a religious icon. *The Garden of Paradise* (c. 1410–20), a painting by an unknown Rhenish artist, shows the Virgin Mary and various saints performing daily tasks in a garden that blooms with many different recognizable flowers, including the Madonna lily and lily of the valley. By the second half of the sixteenth century, the period when all kinds

Plaque depicting
King David with
lilies of the valley.
c. 1594. Bohemia.

of exotic plants were arriving in western Europe from the Ottoman Empire, the gardens of the rich and powerful from Vienna to Rome became an encyclopedic array of flowers. They were conceived, Hobhouse explains, 'as contemporary notions of the original Garden of Eden in which all God's plants, flowering and fruiting at the same time in a sort of perpetual spring, were gathered together'.[6]

A similar picture of abundance is portrayed in the Unicorn Tapestries, a group of seven large wall-hangings that were woven in Brussels about 1500 and are installed at the Cloisters, part of the Metropolitan Musuem of Art in New York City. They depict the ancient myth of the hunt of the unicorn which, according to one interpretation, is an allegory of Jesus's death and resurrection. In the final and most famous scene, the pure white unicorn, bloodied by the hunters, is encircled by a fence and stands on a lawn studded with flowers, including lilies of the valley and prominently tall stems of white Madonna lilies.

In Renaissance portrayals of male and female saints alike – St Francis, St Anthony of Padua, St Anne, St Catherine of Siena – a stem of white Madonna lilies is the prominent symbol of their purity. But

Flemish engraving of
St Francis holding a
lily, c. 1630–75.

its pre-eminent use in Renaissance art is in depictions of the Annunciation, the beginning of Mary's entry into holy motherhood. In painting
after painting, the Archangel Gabriel appears before Mary, not with
garlands or crowns of flowers reminiscent of Roman paganism but with
a single stem of white lilies, as a symbol of the miraculous birth to come.
The scene appears in the masterpieces of every European country
from the early to the late Renaissance: by the south Netherlandish
painter Jan van Eyck; the great Italian artists Leonardo da Vinci, Fra
Filippo Lippi, Sandro Botticelli and Giorgio Vasari; and many others
from Albrecht Dürer to El Greco. Lilies also appear in many other
Renaissance paintings of the Virgin. They stand like sentinels on
either side of Mary's throne in Botticelli's Bardi Altarpiece, the *Virgin
and Child Enthroned between St John the Baptist and St John the Evangelist* (1484).

French etching of the Annunciation, 1613–16, an unusual depiction of the angel Gabriel as a woman.

In Lippi's *Coronation of the Virgin*, the heavenly sky is filled with lilies. The lilies in many Renaissance paintings literally avoid the issue of sexuality: their pistils and stamens, so prominent in the natural world, are either barely visible or completely absent. The great exceptions are Leonardo and Dürer, whose Annunciation paintings and drawings depict *L. candidum* with unmistakable accuracy. Certainly for Leonardo, the indigenous and prolific flower of the Mediterranean must have been a readily accessible model.

Pre-Raphaelite paintings of the mid-nineteenth century continued the tradition of lilies in scenes of the Annunciation. Their renderings of the flower and the Virgin followed the charge of the era's influential

Francesco Vanni (*c.* 1565–1610), *St Catherine of Siena*, fresco.

art critic John Ruskin to be 'true to nature'. In Dante Gabriel Rossetti's *Ecce Ancilla Domini* (Behold the Handmaid of the Lord; 1849–50), Mary is a young girl, shrinking in her bed before the Archangel Gabriel as he hands her a single stem with three white lilies, symbolizing the Holy Trinity. A stem with three lilies is also embroidered on the banner next to Mary's bed. She is seen embroidering this banner in Rossetti's companion painting, *The Girlhood of Mary Virgin* (1848–9). Mary also appears as a shy young woman in Arthur Hughes's *Annunciation* (1857–8). Interrupted from her task of spinning yarn, she leans backward with her head tilted down in awe and perhaps fear at the presence of the archangel, who hovers over a bed of white lilies in the doorway of her chamber. The Pre-Raphaelite association of lilies with virginal purity was so strong that young girls of this period, no matter what

Girl with lilies
dressed for her
First Communion,
1930, photograph.

their religion, were often photographed in white dresses, holding white lilies.[7]

Another Pre-Raphaelite artist, Edward Burne-Jones, portrayed the Annunciation quite differently in his allegorical *The Flower Book* (1882–98). Created for his own pleasure and respite from his other work, this album of tiny watercolour roundels – each about 6 inches (15.2 cm) across – illustrates the Latin names of the flowers in imaginative scenes from Christian tales and medieval legends. Although he had painted several traditional Annunciation scenes, he was after more magical creations in the last decades of his life. His 'White Garden', the *Flower Book* illustration for *L. candidum*, is more like a fairy tale than a religious painting. White lilies fill the background like stars in the night sky. The album also includes 'Ladder of Heaven', an

Edward Burne-Jones, 'White Garden', drawing of the Annunciation in a garden of lilies, from *The Flower Book* (1882–98).

illustration of *Convallaria majalis*, lily of the valley. The flower's tiny blooms, like steps rising up the stem, lend themselves to this metaphor. But rather than a realistic portrayal, Burne-Jones's illustration shows 'A soul climbing the side of a rainbow'. His concept of a picture was 'a beautiful romantic dream of something that never was, never will be – in a light better than ever shone – in a land that no one can define or remember, only desire and the forms divinely beautiful'.[8]

Two very unusual portrayals of the Annunciation were created by the Surrealist artist Salvador Dalí in the mid-twentieth century. Although the treatment is radically different from earlier works by other artists, Dalí's versions keep the traditional stem of lilies. A water-colour of 1947 includes two angels painted in an impressionistic melange of colour, each holding a single stem of lilies. In a drawing of 1956 – perhaps the most unique Annunciation scene of all – the effect is an explosion of black lines. Gabriel and Mary are barely visible, but the stem of lilies is clearly intact.

Simply Pure

Lilies have long been associated with purity and femininity in secular contexts. A poster for the *New York Times* in 1896 depicts a young woman in a white dress holding a white lily, with the title 'The Model of Decent and Dignified Journalism'. The association of lilies with young females is carried over in sporting events today – even when the athlete is an animal. While male horses predominate in the Kentucky Derby, only fillies or female horses run in the Kentucky Oaks, the annual event for three-year-old thoroughbreds that also takes place in Churchill Downs, Louisville. While the horse that wins the Derby is decorated with a garland of roses, the filly that wins the Oaks receives a garland of lilies. The Derby is called the 'Run for the Roses', and ever since it began in 1875 the Oaks has been known as 'Lillies for the Fillies'.

Lilies also accompany young women in many Chinese paintings as a sign of purity and femininity. The association still has currency,

'The Model of Decent and Dignified Journalism', poster for the *New York Times*, 1896. A war of sensational journalism was waging between other New York City newspapers when the *Times* chose this image to proclaim its ethical approach to presenting the news.

since one of the most popular names today for Chinese girls is Lily. Yet its history has a darker side. Chinese women learned how to bind their daughters' feet by practising on a tiny teaching model called a 'lily foot'.

In Japan, lilies were often painted or embroidered on kimonos used by young women in rites of passage and passed down through the generations. The 'Kimono with Carp, Water Lilies and Morning Glories' (*c.* 1876), in the collection of the Metropolitan Museum of Art, New York, was worn by the donor's grandmother for her *jusan mairi*. The ceremony, literally the 'thirteenth temple visit', involves the blessing of thirteen-year-old boys and girls as they enter adolescence.[9]

Throughout the nineteenth century, poets saw pure white lilies as symbols of innocence, perhaps none more so than the simple lily of the valley, of which William Cullen Bryant (1794–1878) wrote:

Japanese actor playing a woman and holding a lily, *c.* 1706–63, woodblock print.

A 'lily foot', a teaching model for Chinese footbinding, *c.* AD 618–906.

> Innocent child and snow-white flower!
> Well are ye paired in your opening hour:
> Thus should the pure and the lovely meet,
> Stainless with stainless, and sweet with sweet.

Walter Crane portrays lilies of the valley as young women in his illustration for the children's book *Flora's Feast* (1895). These 'white ladies delicate and pale' modestly cover their bodies with the flowers' broad leaves. Growing in shaded places, the lily of the valley was seen as a model of modesty for women. A handbook of matrimony from around 1829, *The Matrimonial Preceptor: Instructive hints for those who are, and those who are like to be married*, offers this advice to young women: 'the lily of the valley, less exposed to observation, escapes unhurt, and uninjured

Mary Louise MacMonnies, *Rose and Lilies*, 1897, oil on canvas. The lilies surrounding the mother and child reflect the innocence of the scene.

by the spoiler's hand. Learn, fair daughters of Beauty, from the lily to court the friendly shade.' In his poem *Endymion*, John Keats describes lilies of the valley as 'valley-lilies whiter still / Than Leda's love' (lines 157–8). By alluding to the erotic myth of Zeus, who took the form of a great white swan to ravish Leda, Keats implies that the beauty of nature is purer than sexual love.

Even the calla lily, the sensationally sexual flower of early twentieth-century art, started out as a symbol of female innocence. It frequently appeared in portraits of wealthy matrons of the mid-nineteenth century. 'The lily's perfect form and its whiteness echoed the feminine beauty and unblemished virtue' of these subjects, according to Charles Eldredge in his essay 'Calla Moderna: Such a Strange Flower'. Romantic, at times overwrought poetry of the era confirmed this image. According to the American poet James Gates Percival (1795–1856), the calla's

> . . . beauty should be worshipped,
> And not a thought of weakness or decay

Walter Crane, vase with maidens and lilies, 1906, red earthenware painted with gold
lustre. The mythological scene depicts the daughters of Hesperus dancing around
a tree with golden apples while branches of lilies, nearly as tall as the tree, stand
between them.

Frederick Sandys, *Young Woman with Lilies*, c. 1880, pencil and coloured chalk.
The drawing is believed to show Florence Emily Hesketh, daughter of the senator
of Nevada, and to have been made to celebrate her marriage to an English lord.
The white lilies proclaim her purity, while the snake bangle on her wrist alludes to
Eve in the Garden of Eden and to fertility.

Should mingle with the pure and hallowed dreams
In which it dwells before us.[10]

The painting *Lotus Lilies* (1888) by Charles Courtney Curran (1861–1942) is a serene view of two women in a boat surrounded by yellow water lilies. Dressed in beautiful summer clothing, the women are pictures of feminine beauty, totally different from the sinister depiction of the anthropomorphic water lilies in *Hylas and the Nymphs*. The scene, set on an estuary of Lake Erie in Ohio, is a realistic portrait of the painter's new bride and her cousin, one that held personal significance for the artist since the bride carried a bouquet of water lilies during their wedding ceremony that summer. The lush flowers reflect the women's beauty. The painting is similar to Japanese prints of women gathering lotus flowers, images that Curran might have seen in this age of *Japonisme*. Rather than lotuses, however, which grow in profusion in parts of Asia, the yellow flowers in Curran's painting are probably spatterdock, native water lilies of North America.

S. D. Erhart, 'The Rivals', cover of *Puck* (1905). A stand of white lilies next to the woman emerging from church on Easter morning attests to her chaste beauty. Her purity is further depicted by the devilish figure (right) being turned away.

Monet's water lilies also convey a sense of pure beauty. Capturing the ever-changing play of light on his lily pond was the intense focus of his work in the last three decades of his life. In several late paintings he erased all references to the bank of the pond and to the horizon, creating a virtual sky of water lilies, or what Marcel Proust called 'a celestial garden' in *À la recherche du temps perdu.*[11] Monet painted on large-scale panels and envisioned them lining the walls of an oval room to surround the viewer. In his notes, he wrote of creating a place where 'nerves weighed down by work would be relaxed' and where one could experience 'the asylum of peaceful meditation in the midst of a flowered aquarium'.[12] Although his plans for a dedicated museum in Paris were never realized, 22 of the large panels were permanently installed in the Musée de l'Orangerie in Paris, a space that the Surrealist painter André Masson described as 'the Sistine Chapel of Impressionism'.[13] Monet was an agnostic, but through his radiant water lilies he created a secular environment for sensual immersion in pure beauty that is comparable to a religious experience.

Charles Courtney Curran, *Lotus Lilies*, 1888, oil on canvas.

Suzuki Harunobu (1725–1770), *Two Women Gathering Lotus Flowers*,
woodblock print.

This entry in the Paris body-painting championship in 1996 clearly conveys the sensual appeal of lilies. It is difficult to imagine another flower — a petunia or a pansy, for example — creating the same effect.

seven

The Sexiest Flower

🙼

The early Christians were on to something when they feared that flowers were all about sex. While they banned them from Christian worship in a rejection of Roman idolatry, consciously or subconsciously they must have sensed, as Jack Goody simply states, that:

> Sexuality is the core of the flower's existence. It is the plant's reproductive organ, coloured and perfumed to attract insects that spread the pollen and permit fertilization . . . The very word 'flower' is a sexual metaphor in several languages, as in deflowering a virgin . . . leading to her blossoming forth as a woman.[1]

More than any other garden flower, lilies flaunt their sexuality. Consider the physicality of the true lily. Its erect stamens, each one bearing pollen, the flower's sperm, surround the pistil at the centre of the flower, the entry to the ovary deep within the petals. Linnaeus, who classsified plants according to their reproductive parts, described the lily's six stamens as the flower's 'six husbands', and called the flower head the 'bridal bed'.[2] The u-shaped channel on the inner surface of the petals provides support and a guide for the proboscis of pollinating insects. As Oscar Wilde said in his poem 'Athanasia' (1879), 'the bee [is] the lily's paramour'. Its heady scent is also a defining characteristic, an essence first captured in perfumed oils by the ancient Egyptians and worn by such powerful women as Hatshepsut, the first female pharaoh, Cleopatra and Catherine de' Medici, queen of France in the sixteenth century.[3] Fragrance was another sensuous quality that made Puritans wary of all flowers. Even after the Restoration of the British monarchy in 1660, a bill was introduced in Parliament declaring marriages null and void that had been based on 'female seduction with scents'. The Puritans in the American colonies also associated scents with sexuality: in Pennsylvania, wearing perfume was considered witchcraft.[4]

In the Sermon on the Mount, Jesus cited the lilies of the field as an example of unadorned beauty and simplicity: 'Consider the lilies how they grow: they toil not, they spin not . . . Solomon in all his glory was not arrayed like one of these' (Matthew 6:29). Yet throughout history, the lily has also been the inspiration for radically different ways to consider this flower. Far from the Christian ideal of purity, some stories tie the origin of the lily to original sin. It sprang from the tears of Eve as she left the Garden of Eden, according to a Semitic legend. On a parallel note in Islamic legend, the rose was formed from a tear of the Prophet, but the story has none of the implications of sin of the lily. The biblical love poem the Song of Songs includes lily metaphors that have been interpreted with a wide range of meaning. While the phrase 'the lily among thorns' became a symbol of both Christ and the Virgin Mary, the poem is also rife with erotic lily metaphors expressing the physical desire between a bridegroom and his bride. The bride compares her lover's lips to 'lilies dripping sweet smelling myrrh'. The bridegroom proclaims: 'Thy two breasts are like two young roes that are twins, which feed among the lilies . . . Thy navel is like a round goblet, which wanteth not liquor: thy belly is like a heap of wheat set about with lilies.' The eroticism of these lines has roots in the sensuality of ancient Middle Eastern poetry, yet Christian scholars have interpreted the Song of Songs to be a dialogue of spiritual desire by the soul, represented by the bride, for Christ, the bridegroom. But with metaphors as graphically physical as these, the theory, to the modern secular mind, sounds like revisionist history.

Charles Hurault, photograph. The pronounced stamens and anthers projecting from the centre of the lily are an invitation to pollinating insects and birds.

Nymphs handing lilies to Alexis, 1840, illustration of Virgil's *Eclogue II*,
pen and brown ink. In Virgil's pastoral poem, Alexis is also the object
of a shepherd's homoerotic love.

Amaryllis, the belladonna lily, is the name of the 'wanton country
maid' in the playfully suggestive lute song by Thomas Campion (1567
–1620). Like her namesake, the shepherdess in Virgil's *Eclogues*, she is
an unpretentious peasant girl whom Campion much prefers over more
sophisticated ladies:

> I care not for these ladies that must be wooed and prayed;
> Give me kind Amaryllis, the wanton country maid.
> Nature Art disdaineth; her beauty is her own.
> Her when we court and kiss, she cries: foorsooth, let go!
> But when we come where comfort is, she never will say no.

If I love Amaryllis, she gives me fruit and flowers;
But if we love these ladies, we must give golden showers.
Give them gold that sell love, give me the nut-brown lass.
Who when we court and kiss, she cries: forsooth, let go!
But when we come where comfort is, she never will say no.

These ladies must have pillows and beds by strangers wrought.
Give me a bower of willows, of moss and leaves unbought,
And fresh Amaryllis with milk and honey fed,
Who when we court and kiss, she cries: forsooth, let go!
But when we come where comfort is, she never will say no.

Although Campion was probably inspired by Virgil rather than the actual flower, he would have been amused to know that it is also known as 'the naked lady' because it blooms on a bare stem after the foliage has died.

In the mid-seventeenth century, a time when white lilies were still a popular symbol of purity and innocence, Robert Herrick's poem 'The Lily in a Crystal' (*c*. 1630) made the flower a metaphor for a woman's hidden passion:

> So though y'are white as swan or snow
> And have the power to move
> A world of men to love,
> Yet, when your lawns and silks shall flow,
> And that white cloud divide
> Into a doubtful twilight, then,
> Then will your hidden pride
> Raise greater fires in men.

Two centuries later, the poet Emily Dickinson also explored the lily's complex combination of purity and sensuality. On the surface, the poet seemed to be the picture of virginal innocence. She dressed in white, never married and led a reclusive life, rarely venturing from her home in Amherst, Massachusetts. In her treasured gardens, she grew many flowers and closely identified with them, but 'for the cultivated lily and rose, she reserved a passionate attraction', according to Judith Farr in *The Gardens of Emily Dickinson*.[5] Shy to a fault, she introduced herself to Thomas Higginson, the man who would become her literary mentor, by handing him two lilies from her garden. The gesture, an observer remarked, recalled Oscar Wilde, well known even in Amherst for his signature lily. But Dickinson had probably never heard of him, much less anything of his scandalous behaviour. Dickinson's life recalls the ancient image of a virgin in an enclosed garden, one also described in the Song of Songs: 'A garden locked is my sister, my spouse; a spring shut up, a fountain sealed.' But her poetry and letters are laced with lily symbolism that reveals an inner ardour. Although Dickinson and Wilde were worlds apart in every way, they shared an artistic attraction to sensual Catholic iconography. In *The Passion of Emily Dickinson*, Farr explains that the poet, like many Victorian maidens, was strongly influenced by the sensuous portrayals of the Virgin Mary in Pre-Raphaelite paintings and their emphasis on the lily as the Virgin's emblem. Even for Protestants, 'The nun in white was a seductive figure and the lily associated with her had an erotic perfume.'[6] Farr explains the seeming contradiction:

> In her allusions to herself as a nun, by her assumption of white and her repeated association of herself with lilies, Emily Dickinson was participating in a finely articulated iconographic tradition. It is telling, moreover, that Dickinson carried lilies that were often not white but orange-red, like her hair. In the Victorian palette, red was the colour of passion and suffering. Dickinson once called herself a 'cow-lily', consenting to the tradition whereby unmarried girls were associated with lilies but insisting on the distinction provided by her own colouring and – perhaps – nature; the wayward nun, the artist-recluse.[7]

As a 'wayward nun', Dickinson once said that the only command-ment she followed was to 'consider the lilies'. And while her poetry often employed Christian images of Christ and Heaven, many of her letters and poems are also filled with passionate love for her sister-in-law Susan Gilbert Dickinson. In 'The Waking Year', she writes of two flowers, 'A Lady red . . . a Lady white . . . In placid Lily sleeps'. They awaken in the spring like an unexpected resurrection that shocks 'The tidy Breezes, with their Brooms . . . The Neighbors do not yet suspect!' Scholars debate whether or not they had a lesbian relationship, or simply a strong emotional attachment, common among Victorian women. After years of expressing fervid love for Susan, Dickinson sent a letter using the traditional symbols of the lily and the rose to signal a change in the relationship: 'Take the Key to the Lily now, and I will lock the Rose.' The message was an acknowledgement that Dickinson would lock up her physical passion, symbolized by the rose, and in its place give Susan the key to the lily, or spiritual admiration.[8]

Lilies can be a symbol of heterosexual, homosexual and even bi-sexual love. Oscar Wilde, who cultivated the image of the dandified aesthete – long hair, knee breeches, silk stockings and a velvet coat with a white lily in the lapel – embodied them all. Married with children, he also had many homosexual relationships, including the long-standing one that led to his public downfall. In his lifestyle and writings, the lily conveys a complex combination of aestheticism, Catholic icon-ography and sexuality. During his days at Trinity College in Dublin, Wilde wrote the poem 'Wasted Days', describing a 'fair slim boy' with 'Pale cheeks whereon no kiss hath left its stain'. Years later he rewrote the poem, changing the boy to a 'Lily-girl' with 'Pale cheeks whereon no love hath left its stain' and the title to 'Madonna Mia'. In 'Ave Maria Gratia Plena' he writes of the coming of Christ and evokes the traditional scene of the Annunciation in a more earthly setting:

> Some kneeling girl with passionless pale face,
> An angel with a lily in his hand,
> And over both the white wings of a Dove.

At Oxford Wilde filled his rooms with lilies and pictures of the Virgin Mother. He fashioned his flamboyant appearance in part to shock those who espoused conventional morality and reinforced the effect with his repartee. When during a tour of America in 1882 he was asked about reports that he had paraded down Piccadilly carrying a lily with his long hair flowing, he replied: 'It's not whether I did it or not that's important, but whether people believed that I did.'[9] As he became famous, the press seized on Wilde's appearance and made a fetish of his signature lily. In a notable example, a popular periodical caricatured him in 1880 as the 'Bard of Beauty' with lilies growing at his feet, a perverse comparison to the image of Christ on the cross with lilies at the base. But the comparison would prove prophetic, for Wilde would die on the cross of condemnation for his behaviour. At the height of his popularity as a playwright in 1895, he was tried and convicted for sodomy and sentenced to two years' hard labour. His health and career suffered during imprisonment, and his physical and mental decline eventually led to his death in 1900.

Walter Crane's anthropomorphic lilies at times took explicitly sensuous forms in his children's books of the late nineteenth and early twentieth centuries. In *Queen Summer: The Journey of the Lily and Rose* (1891), he resolves the conflict between the flowers with a similar light-hearted narrative to that employed by William Cowper in his poem a century earlier. But in Crane's fairy tale, of a medieval joust between followers of the lily and the rose, the lily's trumpeters are dressed like calla lilies with the flower's phallic-like spadix protruding from their trumpets and caps. Crane's text reinforces the image: 'The silver arum trumpets sound with tongues of gold.' The lily knight's garments have white, draping sleeves and hems like lily petals, and his lily cap is topped by the flower's pistil and stamens. To begin the duel with the rose he extends his glove, shaped like a lily, to his challenger. Several of the lilies in Crane's *Flora's Feast* take highly sensuous female form. The tiger lily is a woman with bared breasts rising out of a flower as tigers leap from the orange blooms below her. Women are draped languidly over lily leaves in the illustration 'When Lilies of the Day are Done'.

The Water Lily, 1854, etching. A young woman reclining seductively in a pond of water lilies, which add to the sexual implications of the scene.

Water lilies are also portrayed as seductive females in other late nineteenth-century art and poetry. In Stéphane Mallarmé's impressionistic prose poem 'The White Water Lily' (1885), the narrator visits a lily pond and is haunted by the image of a woman he perceives in a white water lily. He says he would gladly be 'enslaved' by this woman, but he plucks the lily and escapes. Echoing Mallarmé's poem, there are some actual water lilies that seduce and entrap the creatures attracted to their colour and scent. The flower of the fragrant water lily *Nymphae odorata* releases a fluid filling the deep centre of the bloom. The design of the petals causes insects alighting on the flower to fall into the fluid. If the insect is covered in pollen from another flower, the pollen dissolves in the fluid and fertilizes the flower. The insect may emerge unharmed, but unlucky ones are trapped and drown. After pollination, the flower stem tightens in a spiral, like a spring, pulling the flower head underwater. The fruit develops there into a spongy berry with many seeds. When ripe, the berry releases up to 2,000 seeds, which float and are dispersed by water currents and birds. As they become waterlogged, they sink into the mud, where they germinate.[10] The entrapment is eerily similar to the image of the young boy pulled into the pond by water lilies in Waterhouse's mythological painting *Hylas and the Nymph* (see p. 105).

Calla Mania

The white calla lily appears in the work of several artists of the late nineteenth century, with different degrees of sexual intensity. While it was primarily a symbol of femininity in paintings of this era, in a few notable exceptions cited by the art scholar Charles Eldredge in his essay 'Calla Moderna', it was part of a highly sensual portrayal. In nineteenth-century art, women, especially those coupled with lilies, were often symbols of spiritual inspiration. But in these examples, they seem to inspire something more down to earth. The full-length female nude in William-Adolphe Bouguereau's *L'Aurore* (1881) is a voluptuous figure as she balances on one foot and bends over to inhale the fragrance of a tall calla lily. *At the Water's Edge* (1894), a painting by Bouguereau's pupil and later his wife, Elizabeth Gardner, suggests a lesbian relationship between the two young women embracing while one reaches to grasp the calla lily growing by the water's edge. Another couple of *fin-de-siècle* artists, Charles Walter Stetson and his wife, Grace Ellery Channing, created a strange painting and tale centred around calla lilies. Working in Pasadena, California, where calla lilies were in wide commercial production during the 1890s, they saw the flowers all around them. Sensual women are absent in Stetson's painting *An Easter Offering* (1896), but the effect of his field of callas blooming in an eerie midnight setting is highly emotive. In the tale written by his wife the same year, *The Madness of the Rector*, calla lilies take on a graphically sexual role. It is the story of a priest's abandonment of his faith in a field of calla lilies on Easter morning. The priest has a sexual awakening in the field while the 'golden tongues' in the 'white throats' of the callas shout 'He is risen! He is risen!'[11]

The calla lily blossomed in the 1920s as an image of overt sexuality, at a time when Sigmund Freud's theories were having a resounding impact and the topic of sex was more widely and freely discussed. In this age of artistic experimentation and departure from conventional art forms, the flower became the focus of a new generation of painters and photographers, often with sexual overtones. In Marguerite Zorach's *New England Family* (c. 1917–20) a potted calla lily placed between a stiff New England couple raises its oversized spadix like a rebellious child sticking out its tongue, or even worse, raising its middle finger. The calla lily was the sole subject of works by Marsden Hartley, Charles Demuth, Joseph Stella, Man Ray and many others. The calla's sculptural beauty alone was fascinating to many artists, apart from any sexual implications. Yet more than any other lily, the calla's physical form – its deep, curving concavity and fleshy spadix suggesting both male and female genitalia – evoked sexual interpretations. And more than any other artist of the period, Georgia O'Keeffe's close-ups of the flower's interior emphasized these features and became her most famous and infamous works. While O'Keeffe dismissed the sexual

Bette Davis in a luxurious gown printed with large calla lilies, 1937.

147

A calla lily: the flower's spadix embraced by its curved petals inspired a
sexual interpretation in countless works of art.

commentary, the reaction by the press reached fever pitch. One of
the most memorable was a caricature by the Mexican artist Miguel
Covarrubias, who drew her in the New Yorker in 1929 as 'Our Lady of
the Lily'. Holding the single stem of a calla lily, she was a wry allusion
to the holy Virgin. O'Keeffe's husband, Alfred Stieglitz, increased
the attention. He arranged the sale of six of her calla lily paintings
for $25,000 in 1928 – more than any other group of contemporary
paintings had sold for up until then. Although the sale fell through two
years later, the publicity made the spotlight on the calla paintings even
more glaring. While promoting the sexuality of her work, he maintained
that the whiteness of the lilies in her paintings was surreal rather than

opposite: Georgia O'Keeffe, *Calla Lily on Grey,* 1928, oil on canvas. One of O'Keeffe's
paintings of calla lilies that attracted controversy for their suggestive nature.

sexual. He referred to them, perhaps with tongue in cheek, as the 'Immaculate Conception'.[12]

O'Keeffe was loath to accept sexual interpretations of her work for several reasons. She felt that they pigeonholed her as a woman rather than accepting her as an artist, and ignored her dedication to higher aesthetic ideals. In his essay 'The Pale Beauty of Priceless Flowers', James Moore, director of the Albuquerque Museum, explains this dilemma for the artist. Going beyond the sensational reactions to O'Keeffe's paintings, he suggests that her work was influenced by more abstract, philosophical concepts. One of these was the influence of the Chinese and Japanese principle of masculine and feminine duality in the natural world. A close friend of O'Keeffe and Stieglitz, Claude Bragdon, had written extensively on this subject and, according to Moore, might have influenced her way of looking at the calla lily. In the following description of the flower, Bragdon uses the Japanese terms *in* for the feminine principle and *yo* for the masculine:

> A calla, consisting of a single straight and rigid spadix embraced by a soft and tenderly curved spathe, affords an almost perfect expression of the characteristic differences between Yo and In and their reciprocal relation to each other. The two are not often combined in such simplicity and perfection in a single form.[13]

The theory of masculine–feminine duality is an intriguing analysis of O'Keeffe's calla lilies. As a universal concept, it also recalls the Greek myths of the lily as a symbol of self-fertilization.

Calla lilies are also a powerful presence in striking paintings by the Mexican artist Diego Rivera. Rather than focusing on botanical realism, he conveys a sense of earthly physicality by pairing massive bunches of the pure white flowers with large, colourful and simplified figures. Rivera was known for his massive murals of historic and political themes, but in his easel paintings of the 1940s calla lilies comprise the most memorable imagery. A South African import, the calla lily

Diego Rivera, *Nude with Calla Lilies*, 1944, oil on board. Rivera often contrasted white calla lilies with dark-skinned figures, conveying sensuality and commenting on the racial mixing between Europeans, Africans and indigenous peoples in the history of the Mexican people.

was a symbol to Rivera of the role that African slavery had played in the racial make-up of the Mexican people.[14] In many cases, Rivera contrasted the white lilies with the dark-skinned indigenous peoples and people of mixed descent who worked as flower vendors. But the flowers also conveyed a strong sense of sensuality in his paintings of both native Mexicans and European settlers. Rivera's own racial heritage was mixed Mexican and European. In *Nude with Calla Lilies* (1944), the nude, dark-skinned female, seen kneeling from behind, embraces and seems to merge with an immense basket of callas. In *Portrait of Mrs Natasha Gelman* (1943), the profusion of calla lilies reinforces the sexuality of the subject, a beautiful, blond woman, the wife of Jacques Gelman, a Russian who became a movie mogul in Mexico. Dressed in a white, tightly fitting, low-cut gown, Mrs Gelman's body is extended along a green sofa. Bunches of callas are behind her, curving down the contours of her body. Their long green stems, white blooms and yellow centres echo her colours and sinuous form.

Not surprisingly, two twentieth-century artists known for their use of sexual themes, Salvador Dalí and Robert Mapplethorpe, produced some of the boldest examples of the calla lily's use as sexual symbol. Dalí's *The Great Masturbator* (1929) is a nightmarish portrayal of a fellatio fantasy. The artist's distorted profile, looking down, fills the canvas. At the back of his neck, a woman's head and shoulders rise like a figurehead with long neck and flowing hair. Her face, eyes closed, approaches a huge but limp phallus. Resting on her breast, like a badge, is a white calla lily.

Like O'Keeffe, Mapplethorpe produced riveting close-ups of the calla lily. It was one of the photographer's favourite subjects and also appears on a porcelain plate he designed in 1989, now in the collection of the Brooklyn Museum. His starkly sexual photographs of the calla lily are both precise and erotic, in some views emphasizing the flower's phallic spadix and in others its feminine curves and concave shape. They became even more sensational by association with his homoerotic images, which shocked the public all the more in this time of increasing fear about AIDS. The calla lily photographs were part of Mapplethorpe's highly controversial retrospective, 'The Perfect Moment', held at the Institute for Contemporary Art, Washington, DC, in 1989. One of the images was used for the cover of the exhibition catalogue, suggesting the sexual content within. The explicit depictions of sex acts in many of the exhibition photographs outraged conservative politicians who attacked the exhibit both for its content and because the sponsoring organization was a recipient of public funds. Although the calla lily photographs were not as controversial, one reviewer described the huge pictures as emanating an 'overwhelming sensuality' for the viewer, 'drawing him in, forcing him to acknowledge their primitive sexuality'.[15]

Looking back through the ages, it seems that lilies have been on a roller-coaster ride of intellectual, moral and artistic reactions to sex. Their sexual symbolism in many forms of cultural expression has peaked during times of heightened sexual awareness and openness, and dipped during periods of asceticism and strict moral codes. But even during times of sexual repression, as Oscar Wilde discovered, it could be an effective sign of rebellion against conventional morality. Along with the fuss about Freudian theories, the sexual fervour surrounding the lily has cooled in contemporary art and criticism. Lilies of all kinds, including the controversial calla, appear in countless works by contemporary artists such as Jim Dine (*Calla Lilies, Verona*, 1992) – without any sexual implications. Perhaps we are in a period of jaded indifference. But the lily, one of the sexiest flowers in nature, is always ready to revel in its glorious sensuality.

French Labour Day (*fête du travail*) poster under the Vichy regime of the Second World War. The lily of the valley is a traditional symbol of good luck on May Day in France, but the tiny sprig depicted here looks like a weak symbol of hope.

eight

Matters of Life and Death

❧

To nearly everyone except gardeners, lilies have just two basic associations – funerals and weddings. Because their beauty is fleeting, flowers are inevitably linked with life and death – and lilies have always had a close relationship with both. They were essential at funerals in ancient Egypt, Greece and Rome, as well as in East Asia, both to honour the dead and to mask the smell of death with their strong fragrance. Roman funerals 'demanded masses of blooms', according to Jack Goody, to adorn the corpse, to scatter on the guests at the funeral banquet and to place in the tomb. Lilies were also engraved as a sign of life everlasting on Egyptian and Roman tombs. Long after the funeral, they were part of important customs to memorialize the dead. Families brought fresh flowers, 'especially lilies, roses and violets, to decorate the tombs and show that the dead were still remembered'.[1]

By contrast, Christians and Jews in the Roman Empire rejected the use of flowers at funerals and gravesites, precisely because of their association with Roman religious practices. While Christians later embraced the lily as a sign of the Virgin Mary and the Resurrection, the prohibition against flowers continues today at Orthodox Jewish funerals. Puritans also abjured the comfort of flowers for grieving families, as they did in all religious observances. Despite the promise of Christian resurrection, the lily's strong link to the Virgin made them wary of any association with what they saw as the excesses of Catholicism.

The white lily was a sign of Christian saintliness, and also a powerful symbol of the Last Judgement. In the Middle Ages and the

Albrecht Dürer, *The Last Judgment* (*The Small Passion*), *c.* 1510, woodcut. The lily and sword on either side of Jesus' head symbolize mankind's fate, of Heaven or Hell.

Renaissance, the event was often portrayed by the figure of Jesus with a huge lily and a sword emanating from opposite sides of his head. On the side of the lily, angels led the blessed to Heaven. Under the sword, devils herded sinners into the mouth of Hell. The lily's association with death was also an inspiration for many poets. The seventeenth-century poet Andrew Marvell may be best known today

for 'To his Coy Mistress', a *carpe diem* call to enjoy physical love before
death ends the pleasure. But he also wrote pastoral poetry filled with
the ancient Latin symbolism of lilies and roses. 'The Nymph Complain-
ing for the Death of her Faun' is a lyrical lament for lost love, embodied
by the death of a faun. The faun, a gift from the nymph's unfaithful
lover, is killed by a 'wanton trooper'. Like the faun, the nymph is a victim
of 'false and cruel men', and her description of the faun in her garden
is a poignant picture of an innocent's death:

> I have a garden of my own,
> But so with roses overgrown,
> And lilies, that you would it guess
> To be a little wilderness;
> And all the spring-time of the year
> It only lovèd to be there.
> Among the beds of lilies I
> Have sought it oft, where it should lie,
> Yet could not, till itself would rise,
> Find it, although before mine eyes;
> For, in the flaxen lilies' shade,
> It like a bank of lilies laid.
> Upon the roses it would feed,
> Until its lips e'en seem to bleed
> And then to me 'twould boldly trip,
> And print those roses on my lip.
> But all its chief delight was still
> On roses thus itself to fill.
> And its pure virgin limbs to fold
> In whitest sheets of lilies cold:
> Had it lived long, it would have been
> Lilies without, roses within.

Lilies were also a seductive symbol of death for Romantic poets
like John Keats, who was 'half in love with easeful Death'. The flower's

Sculpture of the tragic lovers Paul and Virginie in a water lily fountain, Capri.
The story of these young lovers was written in 1787 by Jacques-Henri Bernardin
de Saint-Pierre as a parable of two children of nature corrupted by the artificiality
of French upper-class life.

very whiteness could signal the pallor of illness and imminent death.
Keats knew these signs all too well. When he wrote so exquisitely of
'easeful death' in 'Ode to a Nightingale' (1819), his brother, Tom, had
recently died of tuberculosis and he feared that he would die of the
disease as well. In the same year, Keats wrote 'La Belle Dame sans
Merci', in which he seems to identify with a 'knight-at-arms, alone and
palely loitering':

> I see a lily on thy brow,
> With anguish moist and fever dew

The knight dreams of 'pale kings, and princes too, / Pale warriors,
death-pale were they all', and all in the grasp of 'La Belle Dame sans
Merci', the beautiful woman without mercy, a figure of death.

Even the cheerful orange tiger lily, a fixture of British gardens ever
since it was introduced from Japan in 1804, is a harbinger of death in

Tennyson's 'A Spirit Haunts the Year's Last Hours'. Tennyson was only 21 years old when he wrote the poem in 1830, but he immerses himself in the deathly gloom of an autumn garden. In the repeated last lines of both stanzas, the description of the dying flowers rings 'heavily' like a dirge:

> A spirit haunts the year's last hours
> Dwelling amid the yellowing bowers:
> To himself he talks;
> For at eventide, listening earnestly,
> At his work you may hear him sob and sigh
> In the walks;
> Earthward he boweth the heavy stalks
> Of the mouldering flowers:
> Heavily hangs the broad sunflower
> Over its grave i' the earth so chilly;
> Heavily hangs the hollyhock,
> Heavily hangs the tiger-lily.
>
> The air is damp, and hush'd and close,
> As a sick man's room when he taketh repose
> An hour before death;
> My very heart faints and my whole soul grieves
> At the moist rich smell of the rotting leaves,
> And the breath
> Of the fading edges of box beneath,
> And the year's last rose.
> Heavily hangs the broad sunflower
> Over its grave i' the earth so chilly;
> Heavily hangs the hollyhock,
> Heavily hangs the tiger-lily.

Edgar Allan Poe was a great admirer of Tennyson's mournful poem and of the 'pathos' of Marvell's poem of the nymph and the faun:

'How truthful an air of lamentations hangs here upon every syllable!' But Poe used lilies to create nightmarish visions in his poetry and stories. Water lilies were associated with spirits of the dead in the Maya-Naranjo culture of the Americas, which viewed lakes and ponds as entrances to the underworld. While Poe may not have been aware of this connection, his descriptions of water lilies convey a similar sense of dread and desolation. In 'Dreamland' (1844), he writes of

> Lakes that endlessly outspread
> Their lone waters — lone and dead,

The last two lines of the stanza recall Tennyson's lines.

> Their still waters — still and chilly
> With the snows of the lolling lily.

The scene is macabre in Poe's 'Silence — A Fable' (1837). Narrated by a demon, the tale is set in 'a dreary region in Libya by the borders of the river Zaire':

> For many miles on either side of the river's oozy bed is a pale desert of gigantic water-lilies. They sigh one unto the other in that solitude, and stretch towards the heaven their long and ghastly necks, and nod to and fro their everlasting heads. And there is an indistinct murmur which cometh from among them like the rushing of subterrene water. And they sign one unto the other.

The hellish scene is a 'morass of lilies . . . a wilderness of lilies'. The 'pale legions of water-lilies' run through the story until the climax when 'the water-lilies shrieked within their bed'.

In 'To Paint a Water Lily' (1960), the poet Ted Hughes describes a lily pond as a dark underworld, a link between ancient and contemporary worlds — a gentle reminder of Poe's ominous imagery. A dragonfly, like a miniature dinosaur, flies above the pond and lands on a lily. Unlike Poe's shrieking lilies, Hughes's water lily keeps as still 'as a painting, trembling hardly at all / Though the dragonfly alight / Whatever horror nudge her root'.

Poe also wrote lyrical poems about death, notably 'Lenore' (1843), in which a young man refuses to mourn the death of his fiancée because he sees her rising to 'a golden throne beside the King of Heaven'. Rossetti was inspired by the poem and developed the theme in his own poem (1850) and painting of *The Blessed Damozel* (1875–8). Unlike Marvell, who slyly tells his 'Coy Mistress' 'The grave's a fine and private place / But none I think do there embrace', Rossetti portrays a passion that transcends death. The painting shows the beautiful 'damozel' looking down 'From the gold bar of Heaven'. She holds a stem of three white lilies, signifying her purity. At the bottom of the painting, her earthly lover looks up to meet her gaze, dreaming of the day when she will comfort him like the lilies, which 'lay as if asleep / Along her bended arm'. Although angels separate the couple, the painting, as well as the poem, evokes sensual love. Surrounding the damozel are pairs of embracing lovers. And in the poem, the earthly lover imagines that her supple body 'must have made / The bar she lean'd on warm'.[2] As in many other Victorian poems and paintings, the lily blurs the line between purity and sexuality.

The most graphic botanical symbol of sex and death is the *Amorphophallus titanum*, or titan arum, an exotic lily in the same family as callas, but with a huge and highly unusual bloom. Native to the rainforests of Sumatra, it sends up a huge phallus-like spadix that can reach 9 feet tall (2.7 m). But this sexual performance, which has drawn crowds to Kew Gardens, soon reveals why the plant is also called the corpse flower. After blooming, it emanates a foul odour of decomposing flesh, an attraction to the carrion-feeding insects that pollinate the plant.

Victorians had an almost fetishistic fascination with death and its trappings. Black mourning clothes and jewellery, which often encased a lock of the deceased's hair, were worn for a year or more after a death in the family. White lilies were placed in the coffin and on paintings and photographs of the dead. In the mid- to late nineteenth century calla lilies, not Madonna or Easter lilies, were the traditional funeral flowers. They were prominent decorations on Abraham Lincoln's coffin as the funeral cortège travelled from Washington, DC, to his grave in Springfield, Illinois.[3] They also were strewn over the deathbed of Queen Victoria in 1901. In the painting *Queen Victoria on Her Deathbed* (1901), by Sir Hubert von Herkomer, 'the royal corpse assumed the guise of the lily, with Victoria wrapped in a spathe-like shroud from which emerges, like the spadix, her pallid face.'[4] Easter lilies did not become a popular funeral flower until the twentieth century, when they began to be produced commercially for a mass market. Their blooming time at Easter, signifying rebirth and resurrection, is not a natural occurrence but rather a marketing manoeuvre. Planted outside, the bulbs would flower in the summer, but they are forced by nurseries to be ready for the Easter holiday each spring.

In Katherine Mansfield's short story 'The Garden Party', the image of lush canna lilies embodies the mysteries of life, death and sensuality, at the same time contrasting the luxurious home of a privileged family with the meagre cottage of a working-class man. Published in 1922, it was considered one of the first examples of the modern short story. The plot unfolds through the impressions of an adolescent girl, Laura, who has her first encounter with death just as she is beginning to experience her sexual awakening. As her wealthy family prepares to host a garden party, the florist delivers pots of lilies. Their abundance and intense colour have a sexual effect on the girl, making her nearly swoon with pleasure:

> There just inside the door, stood a wide, shallow tray full of pots of pink lilies. No other kind. Nothing but lilies – canna lilies, big pink flowers, wide open, radiant, almost frighteningly alive on bright crimson stems.
>
> 'O-oh . . .' said Laura, and the sound was like a little moan. She crouched down as if to warm herself at the blaze

'Corpse' lily in bloom at Kew Gardens, 1994. The huge tropical flower emanates an odour of decomposing flesh, which attracts the carrion-feeding insects that pollinate it.

of lilies; she felt they were in her fingers, on her lips, growing in her breast.

As the party is about to begin, Laura learns that a labourer who lives just down the road has been killed in an accident, leaving a wife and five young children. Shocked by the news, she urges her mother to cancel the party, but allows herself to be convinced that 'people like that don't expect sacrifices from us'. She stays at the party, torn between guilt and the seductive pleasure of the food and flowers. Afterwards, her mother tells her to take some of the leftover food and lilies to the labourer's family. Laura recoils at the prospect of facing the bereaved widow, but is once again persuaded by her insensitive mother. With the basket of food and lilies on her arm, she enters the labourer's dark cottage and is ushered into the small bedroom where the dead man is laid out. Unmarked by the accident, he appears to be only sleeping: 'He was given up to his dream. What did garden parties and baskets and lace frocks matter to him? He was far from all those things. He was wonderful, beautiful.' She returns home, stunned by the contrast of the day's events. Sobbing and stammering to her older brother, she can express only an inarticulate question: '"Isn't life," . . . But what life was she couldn't explain.'

Lilies are also a reflection of mortality in contemporary poetry. In 'Day Lilies' (2003), Rosanna Warren's description of the 'shriveled' petals of a daylily conveys a piercing sense of loss: '. . . from each crumpled knot / droops a tangle of rough / notes shrunk to a caul of music'. The poem creates a vivid picture of the fleeting beauty of the flower and of the people, now gone, who toiled to plant them in unforgiving soil.

Signs of Life

By its very name, the daylily speaks of fleeting time, but as Ben Jonson (1573–1637) wrote in 'The Turne', its beauty is not soon forgotten:

> A lily of a day
> Is fairer far in May,
> Although it fall and die that night:
> It was the plant and flower of light.

Although daylily blooms last but a day, the plant lasts virtually forever along country lanes and in the fields of old farms. As Warren's poem conveys, the flower is a vital link between passing generations. The lily's passage from bulb to flower in Emily Dickinson's poem 'Through the Dark Sod' is at once a description of the birth of a flower and a symbolic journey of spiritual awakening:

> Through the Dark Sod – as Education –
> The Lily passes sure –

Lilies of the valley, *muguet* in French, signify a *porte bonheur*, literally a bringer of
happiness or a wish for good luck, on cards traditionally sent on 1 May.
French picture postcard, 1900.

Feels her white foot – no trepidation –
Her faith – no fear –

Afterward – in the Meadow –
Swinging her Beryl Bell –
The Mold-life – all forgotten – now –
In Ecstasy – and Dell –

The lily of the valley, at times called Mary's tears in connection with the Crucifixion, is also the May flower of spring, signifying a 'return to happiness' in the Victorian language of flowers. Today, calla lilies, the nineteenth-century mourning flowers, make up sophisticated wedding bouquets, celebrating life, not death.

In the face of death, lilies also express a love of life. Monet painted his water lilies against the backdrop of the horrors of the First World War. Troop trains passed along the railway lines that cut through his garden, and since his son fought in the thick of the battle of Verdun

Claude Monet in his studio at Giverny in front of a panel of the
Nymphaeas (white water lilies), *c.* 1905.

Claude Monet, *The Waterlily Pond*, 1904, oil on canvas.

in 1916, he was painfully aware of the conflict. Even at the start of the war in 1914, he had expressed guilt about his absorption in painting at a time of great hardship for his countrymen: 'I should be a bit ashamed to think about little investigations into forms and colours while so many people suffer and die for us.' But Simon Kelly, curator at the Saint Louis Art Museum, sees Monet's water lily paintings of this time 'in a more positive light, for it involved producing works focused on the revivifying power of nature in the face of destruction and barbarism'.[5] And his paintings have continued to provide comfort for others in times of conflict and death. During the Vietnam War and the bloody attacks on peaceful demonstrators during the civil rights movement, the poet Robert Hayden (1913–1980) described his visits to see Monet's painting of water liles as a beautiful antidote to the 'poisons' of 'Selma and Saigon' ('Monet's Water Lilies', 1968).

The lily was also a popular image of hope during the Second World War. Several months after the United States joined the war, a drawing of an Easter lily, titled 'Imperishable', was published in the *New York Times* (6 April 1942). Surrounded by the raging 'fires of totalitarianism', the lily stood upright, a symbol of confidence that the Allied forces would prevail. Even in German-occupied France, vendors continued to sell lilies of the valley, the traditional symbol of good luck, every 1 May throughout the war.

Pierre Jahan, German officer buying lilies of the valley in Paris during the occupation, 1 May 1941.

Lily tributes placed outside the home of the late Beatle George Harrison
after his death in 2001.

Many contemporary poets have used lily imagery to reflect on life
and death. Thomas Heise does so with black humour. In his poem
'Epitaph x' from his collection *Horror Vacui* (2006), he wants to carry
a calla lily 'Like an umbrella in daylight', placing it 'On the cemetery
gate' and sleeping 'until the groundskeeper found me'. Mary Oliver's
poem 'Lilies', from her collection *House of Light* (1990), is a personal
response to the Sermon on the Mount. She thinks about living 'like
the lilies/that blow in the fields' but does not envy their humble
endurance. Instead she imagines their sexual pleasure at the touch of
a hummingbird. While the poem is a poignant acknowledgement
of short-lived joy and inevitable death, it is also a sensual evocation
of the beauty of nature, 'where the ravishing lilies/melt, without
protest, on their tongues'.

Lily of the Valley, ballet costume by Wilhelm Pantomime Designs, from the *Bell Flower Ballet* performed at Crystal Palace, 1890.

nine
Always Entertaining

꩜

Over the past two centuries, the lily has brought its mixed bag of meanings to songs, theatre, film, children's books and everyday speech. As in mythology, art and literature throughout the ages, lilies in these more recent forms of popular entertainment reflect a wide range of cultural and moral issues, from religion to racial politics and changing trends in comedy and sexuality.

One of America's best-known songs of the nineteenth century, 'The Battle Hymn of the Republic', the Civil War anthem of the North and a present-day standard, carries the age-old religious symbolism in the line, 'In the beauty of the lilies, Christ was born across the sea.' A few years later, the orange tiger lily, a flamboyant contrast to the saintly white lily, made a memorable appearance as a dominant personality in Lewis Carroll's *Through the Looking Glass* (1871). Trying to find her way out of the Garden of Live Flowers, Alice comes upon the flower and has a surprising exchange:

> 'O Tiger-lily', said Alice, addressing herself to one that was waving gracefully about in the wind, 'I wish you could talk!'
> 'We can talk,' said the Tiger-lily: 'when there's anybody worth talking to.'

In mythology and traditional literature, the pure white lily is no match for the passionate rose, but this orange tiger lily is clearly in charge of the garden. She commands the chattering daisies to keep

Georges-Jacques Gatine after Horace Vernet (1789–1863), woman with a lily hat, illustration. Lilies became part of elaborate fashion designs like this 'marvellous number 16' straw hat.

Chandeliers in the shape of water lilies in the Music Room, Brighton Pavilion, 1824. The richly coloured illustration shows a party under way with the Prince Regent seated on the left.

Alice confronts the talking tiger lily, an illustration by John Tenniel from
Lewis Carroll's *Through the Looking Glass* (1871).

quiet – 'Silence, every one of you!' – and contradicts the rose, who
thinks that Alice's face 'has some sense in it' and 'is the right colour'.
'I don't care about the colour', Tiger-lily says. 'If only her petals
curled up a bit more, she'd be all right.'

In the same era, the white lily was a favourite symbol of the Aesthetic
Movement and also the object of its irreverent tributes. The movement, at its height in Britain in the 1870s and 1880s, popularized
the validity of art as a personal perception of beauty apart from any

moral or ethical standards. The concept was embraced by artists as well as many members of the rising middle class who were increasingly patronizing the arts. Both were satirized in Gilbert and Sullivan's comic opera *Patience*, which opened in London in 1881 and toured America the same year. A song published that year, 'My Aesthetic Love or Utterly Utter, Consummate Too Too', included the lines:

> She's utterly consummate too too!
> And feeds on the lily and old china blue.

On the title page of the sheet music was a disconsolate young woman gazing at a blue pot of three lilies.

One of the main characters in *Patience* is the 'fleshly poet' Reginald Bunthorne, based on several Aesthetic poets of the day – Algernon Charles Swinburne, Dante Gabriel Rossetti, also known for his 'fleshly' paintings, and Oscar Wilde. Like Wilde, Bunthorne wears knee breeches and a velvet waistcoat; he carries a lily and sings: 'Let me confess! A languid love for lilies does not blight me!' In 1882 the operetta's producer, D'Oyly Carte, hired Wilde to popularize the production in America through a series of lectures on aestheticism that identified him closely with Bunthorne and fixed the lily as the mark of an effeminate artist. A song published in America that year was 'The Flippity Flop Young Man', with a photo of Oscar Wilde on the sheet music cover. One of the verses was:

> I'm a worship-the-lily young man.
> Crutch and tooth pick-a-dilly young man;
> Cracked in the filberty, Bernard and Gilberty
> Strike you with paper young man.

Highly popular, *Patience* was one of Gilbert and Sullivan's longest running productions, second only to *The Mikado*. Soon after its initial production, it inspired the creation of a Worcester teapot with a male and female aesthete on opposite sides. Both figures have limp wrists,

Cover of the sheet music of the 'Patience Quadrille' from *Patience*, Gilbert and Sullivan's parody of the Aesthetic Movement, featuring the fictional poet Reginald Bunthorne. His signature lily adorns the top left.

forming the spout, and hands on hips, forming the handle. On one side is a long-haired, effeminate male wearing a sunflower (another popular symbol of the Aesthetic Movement) and on the other is a female figure with a calla lily. Only a moustache on the male distinguishes it from the female figure.

At the peak of his popularity as a playwright, Wilde's trademark lily was taken up by his fans. *The Importance of Being Ernest* opened in 1895, his fourth popular West End play in only three years. A snowstorm covered London on opening night, 14 February, St Valentine's Day, but the St James's Theatre was nonetheless packed with the fashionable set. 'As a tribute to Wilde's dandified aestheticism, women wore sprays of lilies as corsages and many young men wore lilies of the valley on the lapels of their tailcoats.'[1] Wilde, too, of course, wore lilies of the valley in the buttonhole of his white waistcoat with black velvet collar. The night was also the start of the scandal that would end Wilde's career and shift the association of his signature lily from aestheticism to homosexuality.

Wilde adored Lillie Langtry, the British actress and darling of the London scene in the 1870s and '80s. She was a favourite model of the Pre-Raphaelite artists John Everett Millais, Edward Poynter, Edward Burne-Jones and Frank Miles, who created the portraits that made her the most famous beauty of the day. While many other female celebrities also bear the name 'Lily' or 'Lillie', no other was so closely associated with the actual flower. Born Emilie Charlotte Le Breton in 1853, she was nicknamed the 'Jersey Lily', both for her birthplace on the island of Jersey in the Channel Islands and for her flawless ivory complexion. Wilde became her close friend, 'christened' her 'Lillie' and persuaded her to become an actress. After her performances, he would shower her with lilies. He displayed a portrait of her by Poynter in the drawing room of his London flat, on an easel surrounded by pots of lilies.[2] Like Wilde, Langtry made the lily her personal emblem. Photos and sketches of her with a Jersey lily (*Amaryllis belladonna*) in her hair were reproduced as postcards and widely circulated. Several were drawn by Miles, who earned his living by sketching celebrities and selling them to publishers. He also grew lilies and even cultivated a new species.[3] Langtry's portrait by Millais, *A Jersey Lily* (1878), which hung in the Royal Academy, shows her holding a Guernsey lily (*Nerine sarniensis*, a South African import of the seventeenth century), since no Jersey lilies were available at her sitting in Covent Garden. Married and divorced several times, she was also the publicly recognized mistress of the Prince of Wales, later Edward VII. After her acting career, she endorsed cosmetics and soap in advertisements, and in 1890 was caricatured in *Punch* sitting on a soapbox and holding a stem of lilies. Some generations after her death, she became the unlikely subject of a song by The Who, 'Pictures of Lily' (1967), a humorous euphemistic tale of childhood masturbation. The father in the song hangs a picture of a

Lillie Langtry, the actress also known as the 'Jersey Lily', gathering lilies, studio photograph, c. late 19th–early 20th century.

Sidney Poitier in a poster for *Lilies of the Field* (1963).

beautiful woman named Lily on the wall of his son's bedroom to help him sleep. The boy falls in love with the picture and asks his father where he can find Lily. Although Langtry is not specifically named in the song, the father explains that the woman in the picture died in 1929 – the same year as Langtry.

A later star of American theatre and film, Katharine Hepburn, uttered a few lines about calla lilies in the film *Stage Door* (1937) that became an iconic piece of movie dialogue. Hepburn plays an aspiring actress in a New York rooming house filled with other young women trying to make a career in Broadway theatre. Through her wealthy father's influence, she is chosen to act in a play and rehearses the lines repeatedly, but unconvincingly. The lines sound hollow, particularly to her competitive and wise-cracking room-mates, played by Ginger Rogers, Lucille Ball and Eve Arden. But once the film's climax takes place – the tragic suicide of one of the house residents – Hepburn recites the lines again with great meaning and resonance: 'The calla lilies are in bloom again. Such a strange flower, suitable to any occasion.

I carried them on my wedding day. Now I place them here in memory of something that has died.'

The American film *Lilies of the Field* (1963), starring Sidney Poitier, recalls the lines from the Sermon on the Mount, but the plot could not be more different than its biblical source. It is the story of a black Baptist man building a Catholic church for a group of East German nuns in the wilds of Arizona. The black-and-white film has dramatic scenes of visual contrast between the dark-skinned actor and the white nuns in their white habits, standing like Christ's lilies in windswept fields. Poitier won the Academy Award for best actor for the film, signalling the acceptance of a black actor in a mainstream film, a milestone in racial relations in the U.S. The film was so successful that it was made into a Broadway musical, *Look to the Lilies*, in 1969.

Speaking of Lilies

Although the lilies Jesus referred to may have been red, the popular image of the 'lilies of the field', both in church and Hollywood, is unmistakably white. *Lilies of the Field* dealt humorously with the cultural and racial contrast between his character and the German nuns, who believe that he was sent to them by God and refuse to pay him for his work, but the role of a black actor in a film with a lily in the tile has ironic implications. It brings to mind the term 'lily-white', a racist distortion of the lily's symbolism of purity, meaning the exclusion of black people. Unfortunately still in use, the term dates to the Lily-White Movement that began within the Republican Party after the American Civil War. As the party of Abraham Lincoln, it had very few supporters in the South. White Republicans, seeking to attract Southern voters, began an organized effort to drive black people from positions of party leadership. The term is thought to have originated at the Republican state convention in Fort Worth, Texas, in 1888, when a group of white supporters tried to expel black delegates. As Paul Casdorph explains in *A History of the Republican Party in Texas, 1865–1965* (1965), the black politician who controlled the state party at the time labelled the insurgents 'lily-whites', and the term took root with similar groups throughout the South. While black people appealed to northern Republican leaders to halt the movement, the Lily-Whites prevailed under Republican presidents until Herbert Hoover's last term ended in 1933. Lily-White domination of the Republican Party became academic during the 1930s because black members joined Democrat Franklin D. Roosevelt's New Deal coalition.

Lily symbolism has also entered popular speech through even older sources. Shakespeare gave the lily's white colour another derogatory meaning. Macbeth calls his servant 'lily-livered' because of his cowardice. While the liver is dark red with blood, Macbeth implies that fear of the approaching English soldiers has drained the servant's liver of blood, making it as pale as his 'linen cheeks' and 'wheyface' (v, iii, 15–17). The term 'lily-livered' is still in use today. John Wayne used it to challenge villains in many western films, setting the stage for similar insults by countless other Hollywood cowboys.

Another popular lily phrase is derived from Shakespeare's *King John*: 'To gild refined gold, to paint the lily . . . is wasteful and ridiculous excess' (IV, ii, 11–16). Although Shakespeare never actually used the words 'gild the lily', the phrase became firmly established in everyday speech. And he may have been inspired by an even older source. Pliny the Elder criticized the practice of making white lilies bear purple flowers by steeping the stalks in red wine: 'There has been invented also a method of tinting the lily, thanks to the taste of mankind for monstrous productions . . . the stalks are left to steep in the lees of black or Greek wine, in order that they might contract its colour.'⁴ Shakespeare may also have been aware of the practice from its description in the popular herbal written by his contemporary John Gerard in 1597: 'if the root be curiously opened, and therein be put some red, blew, or yellow colour that hath no causticke or burning qualities, it will cause the floure to be of the same colour.' The father of plant physiology, the appropriately named Nehemiah Grew (1641–1712), added his criticism in the spirit of Shakespeare's admonition against 'gilding the lily': 'putting the Colour desired in the Flower into the Body or Root of the Plant [is] such a piece of cunning, as for the obtaining a painted Face, to eat a good store of White or Red Lead'.[5] What would they all think of modern hybridizers who now paint the lily in a rainbow of colours?

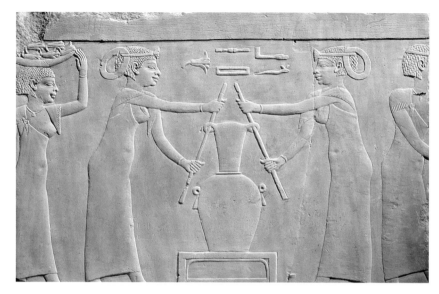

Ancient Egyptian relief showing women squeezing lilies
in a press for perfume, 664–525 BC.

ten

A Lily a Day Keeps the Doctor Away

§

I t is a wonder, considering the sufferings of Job, that he never consulted a herbalist. From ancient Egyptians to modern practitioners of aromatherapy, lilies and many other herbs and flowers have been used as ointments, poultices, tinctures and oils to cure every pain and disease of the body or disturbance of the mind and spirit.

The Chinese have been using lilies as medicine for at least two millennia. The oldest extant Chinese text referring to lilies, the *Divine Husbandman's Classic of Materia Medica*, was compiled no later than the second century BC, but was probably based on earlier writings and traditions.[1] It attributes its knowledge to Shennong, the legendary deity of its title, credited with originating agriculture. The deity is an interesting parallel to the Roman god Mars, revered not only as the god of war but also as the guardian of agriculture because his mother, Juno, became pregnant at the touch of a lily. Chinese herbal medicine, like that of the West, offered cures for everything, including the pains of pregnancy and birth. Herbals from both cultures recommend daylily roots to ease the pain of childbirth and expel the afterbirth. Pregnant Chinese women wore the flowers to ensure the birth of a son. The Chinese also called the daylily 'the plant of forgetfulness', and believed that it was able to cure sorrow as well as pain – not surprisingly, since according to some reports ingesting the plant in large doses can produce a hallucinogenic effect.[2] Chinese herbal medicine today prescribes lily substances for chronic coughing, blood disorders, neurosis and sleeplessness,[3] conditions that ancient herbalists in the West also treated with lilies.

Herbal treatises were being written about the same time in China and ancient Greece. Aristotle was interested in plants as medicine and his pupil Theophrastus, the author of the first systematic classification of plants in Western literature, included their medicinal uses in his treatises. His *Enquiry into Plants* included flora not only from the Mediterranean but also exotics from Egypt, Persia, Arabia and India, brought to him by 'his fellow pupil, Alexander' (later 'the Great').[4] Herbalists were the doctors of the day and the one with the most lasting credibility was the Greek physician Dioscorides, whose treatise of the first century AD on the identification and healing qualities of 500 plants was 'infinitely more impressive than anything that was to be produced for the next one thousand years', according to Wilfrid Blunt in *The Illustrated Herbal*: 'It seems almost incredible that the influence of Dioscorides, who wrote his *De materia medica* in the reigns of Nero and Vespasian, should have persisted until at least the beginning of the nineteenth century.[5] The medical profession almost disappeared after the fall of Rome and was kept tenuously alive by Arabic translators and Christian monks, who laboriously copied the manuscripts of Dioscorides. His work continued as a primary authority on medicine because, for centuries, nothing else took its place.

Two very popular herbals of the seventeenth century, by the barber-surgeon John Gerard (1545–*c*. 1611) and the astrologer-physician Nicholas Culpeper (1616–1654), are combinations of Dioscorides, folklore and remedies handed down verbally throughout the ages. Still in circulation today, they are valuable records of the plants that grew in Elizabethan gardens. And they have much to say about the 'vertues' of several kinds of lilies. Gerard's *Herball*, first published in 1597 and revised in 1633, claims that the Madonna lily bulb, mixed with honey or oil, can mend cuts and also cause hair to grow on bald spots. It is 'full of tough and clammy juice' that 'stamped with hony gleweth together sinues that be cut in sunder . . . It bringeth the hairs again upon places which have been burned or scalded, if it be mingled with oil or grease.' The roots of daylilies, he maintains, may 'be laid with good successe upon burnings and scaldings'.

The ancient authors were 'silent as fishes' about the medicinal properties of lilies of the valley, according to the sixteenth-century botanist Otto Brunfels,[6] but Gerard makes far-reaching claims for the tiny flowers:

> The floures of the Valley Lillie distilled with wine, and drunke the quantities of a spoonefull, restore speech unto those that have the dumb palsie and that are falne into the Apoplexie, and are good against the gout, and comfort the heart. The water . . . doth strengthen the memory that is weakened and diminished; it helpeth also the inflammations of the eies, being dropped thereinto.

Lily of the valley water was 'considered so precious', according to Alice M. Coats, that it was 'kept in vessels of gold and silver'.[7] The plant is poisonous if eaten, but perhaps just a spoonful never killed anyone. Yet Gerard's actual recipe seems almost as bad as the disease:

> The floures of May Lilies put into a glasse, and set in a hill of ants, close stopped for the space of a moneth, and then taken out, therein you shall finde a liquor that appeaseth the paine and griefe of the gout, being outwardly applied; which is commended to be most excellent.

Culpeper's *Complete Herbal*, published in 1653, repeats Gerard's claims and offers additional lily cures for many other painful conditions. Lilies of the valley are 'also of service', he maintains, 'in disorders of the head and nerves, such as epilepsy, vertigo and convulsions of all kinds'. The flowers and roots of the Madonna lily, made into a poultice or bruised and boiled with wine, are recommended for any number of Job-like afflictions:

> they are . . . good to dissolve and ripen hard tumours and swellings . . . and are good antidotes for poison; they are

excellent in pestilential fevers . . . The juice, being baked
with barley-meal and eaten, is good for the dropsy . . . and
ointment made of the roots and hogs' grease . . . cleanses
ulcers . . . and plague sores . . . and is good for swellings in
the privities.

The water lily *Nymphaea odorata*, Culpeper writes, is also equal to any
need, whether medical, mental or sexual:

the syrup of the flowers procures rest, and settles the brains
of frantic persons . . . The seed as well as the root is effectual
to stay fluxes of blood or humours, either of wounds or of the
belly; The root will also cool hot urine if boiled in wine and
water, and the decoction drank . . .

Surprisingly, this highly fragrant water lily, which entices and entraps
insects in its sweet nectar, was also used to control sexual urges. Culpeper
maintains that 'the roots are more effectual to restrain all fluxes in man
or woman . . . and passing away of the seed when one is asleep'. Mixed
with honey, the powdered root was called an *electuaire de chasteté*, a pre-
scription used in Swedish convents and monasteries.[8]

Strange as they may sound today, the medicinal claims made by
Gerard and Culpeper are still popular to some extent in contemporary homeopathic and herbal practices. Published in 1997, *The Book of
Herbal Wisdom: Using Plants as Medicine* follows up some of the old herbal
treatments with its own surprising claims. The author, Matthew Wood,
a 'registered herbalist with the American Herbalist Guild', explains
that he once used a tincture of the Easter lily, an age-old treatment
for respiratory infections, to cure a female stripper with chronic
bronchitis. Another patient, a woman with ovarian cysts, was told
that she could never have children. Within three months of taking the
lily tincture, Wood reports, the cysts were gone and, like Juno at the
touch of Flora's lily, she was pregnant. The disappearing cysts may
seem miraculous, but at least one other type of lily has also been used

Advertisement for French perfume, Au Fil de L'Eau (with the stream, or colloquially, the current fashion), 1926. The water lilies suggest the perfume's aromatic and romantic qualities.

in traditional pharmacology as a treatment for bronchitis. The sea squill (*Urginea maritima*), a member of the lily family found in the Mediterranean and North Africa, has a property that can loosen thick phlegm and is used in some cough medicines today. It also has been used as a diuretic and to treat heart conditions.[9]

As well as curing diseases, the roots of water lilies 'boiled in wine and water' was a skincare remedy. Culpeper notes that it 'will also take away freckles, spots, [and] sunburn from the face and other parts of the body'. Dioscorides' recommendation is a face pack made of mashed Madonna lily bulbs mixed with honey.[10] John Parkinson (1567–1650), an apothecary to James I of England and later the head botanist to Charles I, describes a cleanser using the lily's petals: 'The water of the flowers distilled . . . is used . . . of divers women outwardly, for their faces, to cleanse the skin, and make it white and fresh.' Another lily species, *Cloragalum*, was used as soap by Native Americans and early settlers in California. Several species of 'soap lily', which grow in the dry, rocky coast of southern California, contain saponin, a property that foams in water. The leaves and stems were also used by Native Americans as a green dye in tattoos.[11]

According to the Chinese, lilies are beneficial to the *qi*, or vital energy. In today's market for energy drinks and holistic medicine, the claim has a modern ring. It dates, however, from the first government-sponsored pharmacopoeia of China, published in AD 659.[12] The ancient east Indian practice of Ayurveda, still followed today, uses a compound made from the roots of the star water lily, *Nymphaea stellata*, in the treatment of a variety of ills, including liver disorders, diarrhoea, urinary tract and kidney problems and skin diseases. The leaves and seeds are used to treat stomach upsets.

Using lilies for cosmetic purposes also dates from ancient times. Elizabeth Anne Jones traces many of these uses throughout history in her book *Awaken to Healing Fragrances: The Power of Essential Oil Therapy* (1999). 'By 80 BC, the average Egyptian citizen was a connoisseur of fragrance and could find a hundred different oils in the market place.' Lily oil was one of the favourites. Elizabethan households, from Queen Elizabeth's castles to the smallest country houses, had 'still rooms' dedicated to distilling the oils of plants for medicine and perfume. Garden books from this era, Jones says, are full of recipes for 'fragrant Madonna Lily water' and many other distillations of flowers and herbs to scent the body, clothing, bedding and the home.

'Madonna lily' could be an apt name for modern cologne and cosmetics, and might appeal to women who use natural products today. Several historical sources offer 'white water lily lotion' as a skin moisturizer. But beyond purely cosmetic uses, the intense fragrance of lilies has been used for thousands of years to convey a sense of well-being. The ancient Egyptians believed that it was a source of divine powers, as Marina Heilmeyer reports in *The Language of Flowers*: 'On their frescoes, figures are frequently portrayed enjoying the delicious fragrance of blue water lilies. By breathing in the scent, they believed that they were inhaling divine power.'[13]

Conserving lily
petals in alcohol
for perfume,
France, 1920.

Although it may not be the source of divine power, fragrance is
the basis of the positive effects of aromatherapy, Jones explains. She
also cites the use of flowers today as an environmental factor in healing gardens. Hospitals, nursing homes, substance-abuse treatment
centres, hospices and other care facilities have established gardens with
large water lily ponds, bubbling fountains and other naturally calming
features as a supplemental aid to modern medicine. The use of lily
ponds and fragrant flowers recalls the meditative effect of ancient
Islamic gardens and the reflective, immersive beauty of Monet's water
lily paintings. Studies have shown that patients who spend time in
these healing gardens, or whose rooms face them, have positive outcomes
in stress reduction and relief from chronic pain and depression.[14] While
scientists have not identified the specific causes, the peaceful, soothing
surroundings, the gentle sounds of moving water and the fragrant
flowers all seem to have a healing effect on body and mind.

eleven
Lilies on Your Plate

᯽

'Personally, I would as soon turn cannibal as devour a lily.'

So said Alice M. Coats, the British horticultural historian, in noting the Chinese practice of eating lilies. John Veitch, the nurseryman who introduced *Lilium auratum*, the sensational Queen of Lilies, in the nineteenth century, reported that the Japanese boiled and ate the bulbs, 'much as we do potatoes . . . [they] have an agreeable flavour resembling that of a chestnut'. Coats is not alone. Another observer expressed an even stronger distaste for the practice: 'to us the eating of lily bulbs seems as foolish a proceeding as the eating of nightingale's tongues or the dissolving of pearls in vinegar to make sauce for a leg of mutton.'[1]

Yet people throughout history, and even some gardeners, have believed that eating lilies was neither wasteful nor mad. 'What a shame the potato got in the way of the lily as a staple diet', Michael Jefferson-Brown writes in *Lilies: A Gardener's Guide* (1995). 'I could cope with the scent and sight of fields full of lilies.'

The revulsion against eating lilies is a luxury of the well fed. Their bulbs, tubers and rhizomes have an abundant supply of carbohydrates and for thousands of years people throughout the world have foraged for them, particularly in times of famine. Native Americans, Africans and east Indians ate the young leaves and buds of water lilies as vegetables and made flour out of the dried roots and seeds. The bulbs of the camas lily, *Camassia quamash*, were also a staple in the diet of many Native American tribes, but were unknown to settlers

opposite: Gathering the buds of daylilies on a farm in China.

until Meriwether Lewis and William Clark came across them in their westward expedition of 1804–6. Unlike true lilies, camas lilies can be blue. When Lewis and Clark saw thousands in the distance spreading across the plains, they thought they were seeing a lake. They learned to dig and roast the bulbs as did the Native Americans, savouring the sweet-potato taste. They also learned to distinguish them from a similar-looking one, the star-lily *Zigadenus fremontii*, after these 'death camas' caused serious illness to members of the expedition. As white settlers moved west and raised livestock on the prairies, the fields of camas lilies were destroyed, increasing tension with the native tribes. Today, Native and white Americans alike celebrate the flower in the annual Camas Lily Days that take place each summer in Idaho.[2]

Lily bulbs have been cultivated for food in China, Korea and Japan for more than a thousand years. Unlike squeamish gardeners today, the Chinese grew several true lily species for their exquisite form – and also happily ate them. A Chinese agricultural treatise from the tenth century, *Compendium of Essential Tasks for the Four Seasons,* offers advice on fertilizing lilies for food. They were called *bai he,* or 'hundred united', a reference to their segmented, garlic-like bulbs, and were thought to be formed by earthworms knotted together and transformed into plants. But the theory did not inhibit people from eating them, or from appreciating their beauty. The emperor Xuan, a sixth-century ruler of the Liang Dynasty, composed a poem in praise of *bai he*:

> Their leaves cluster layer upon layer;
> Their flowers open immaculate,
> Cupping the dew or downward inclined.
> They sway with the motion of the air.[3]

When Genghis Khan's Mongol invaders turned the cultivated lands of China into horse and herd pastures in the twelfth and thirteenth centuries, the Chinese returned to gathering lily bulbs in the wild, but cultivation resumed in the fourteenth century under the Ming Dynasty – and never ended.[4] Today, the buds and bulbs of daylilies and tiger lilies are an important ingredient in Chinese cuisine.

The sweet fragrance of lilies was important during the Renaissance, Jack Goody explains, because sugar was an expensive import: 'Sugar did not reach the culture of the masses until the late eighteenth century. So where the bee sucked was important to all.'[5] Elizabethan cooks sweetened puddings and cakes with fragrant flower petals – a subtle flavouring that our sugar-laden palettes may not appreciate. In his comprehensive *Paradisus* (1629), listing thousands of plants, John Parkinson prized the Turkish lily for its special sweetness. Known today as the crown imperial or *Fritillaria imperialis*, to Parkinson it was 'the finest of lilies', both for its beauty and sweet nectar: 'At the bottome of the flower next unto the stalke, every leafe thereof hath on the outside a certaine bunch . . . and on the inside there lyeth in those hollow bunched places, certaine cleare drops of water like unto pearles, of a very sweet taste almost like sugar.'

The French gastronome Jean Anthelme Brillat-Savarin (1755–1826) took delight in the sweet fragrance and taste of daylilies, preserved in concentrated form in pastilles or lozenges. In his landmark work *Physiologie du gout* (1825), he describes taking a long walk to a pharmacy in the Faubourg Saint-Germain to purchase the 'rare crystallization': 'First of all I tasted one, and I must be just and say that I found these little pastilles most agreeable; but this made me even more annoyed that, in spite of the outer appearance of the box, they were so few in number.'[6]

Lilies, especially daylilies, can be used as ingredients in many different recipes. Daylily tubers provide a crunch in stir fries, similar to water chestnuts. The dried buds of tiger lilies and daylilies, known as golden needles, are a delicacy traditional in Chinese cooking – quite tasty in soups or sautéed with garlic and pork. There is even a cocktail called the 'Jersey Lily', in honour of Lillie Langtry, and another, the 'Oaks Lily', named for the Kentucky Oaks horse race, although neither drink has any actual lily ingredients. Fresh daylily flowers can

Lily buds, known as 'golden needles', drying in the sun on a large-scale Chinese farm. The dried buds are used extensively in Chinese cuisine and medicine.

be added to salads, sugared as deserts or stuffed and deep-fried like courgette (zucchini) blossoms. Craig and Mary Barnes, owners of Slate Hill Daylilies, a farm in upstate Salem, New York, are fond of eating them raw:

> Sometimes while walking through our fields, we just pop the petals in our mouths. They taste something like Boston lettuce, a little sweeter, like lilacs. The young white nodules of new roots taste like radishes, not quite as spicy, and can be added to salads and stir fries. You can eat the whole plant.[7]

Not only tasty, daylilies also are nutritious, according to the botanist Peter Gail: 'Daylily buds and blossoms have almost as much protein as spinach, more vitamin A than string beans, and about the same amount of vitamin C as orange juice.'[8]

In cooking with daylilies, a few preliminary instructions are essential. Most important, do not use the innocent-looking lily of the valley. Despite Gerard's and Culpeper's medicinal concoctions, all parts of the flower are poisonous if eaten. Another one to avoid is the flamboyant but highly toxic gloriosa lily, also known as the flame lily or climbing lily. Daylilies are your safest bet, but pick the flowers from your own garden, not from the roadside, to ensure that they are free of traffic pollutants and pesticides. As with all flowers, the best picking time is in the early morning before the sun has wilted the blossoms. Pull out and discard the stamens (the pollen could cause allergic reactions), rinse the blossoms to get rid of any hiding bugs, and gently shake them dry. Wrap them loosely in a paper towel and store in a plastic bag in the refrigerator until you are ready to cook. For future use, the buds and flowers can be blanched quickly in boiling water, drained, cooled and frozen. Young daylily leaves can also be sautéed in oil or butter, alone or in combination with other tender greens.

Young tubers, the fat swellings of the roots, are also edible, with these precautions: do not eat the thinner root tissue leading into and out of the tubers. These string-like roots are not edible – in fact, they can be poisonous in large doses. Cat owners should also be wary of all lilies, which are said to be highly toxic for these small animals. Another word to the wise before munching on any raw part of the plant: eat only small amounts at first. Some people have found that they can have a mild laxative effect. Harvest young tubers in spring when they are filled with sugars and starches and produce maximum crunch. In parts of Korea, they are as popular a spring vegetable as asparagus in Western countries. Peter Gail, whose little book provides an appetizing collection of recipes, also advises gardener-cooks to harvest tubers from only the common daylily:

> Since wild-type daylilies are prolific dividers, taking a mess of tubers now and then from any reasonably large patch amounts to nothing more than thinning it. Make sure, however, that you leave enough tubers to start your crop next year! Don't do this with your expensive hybrids. Since they don't divide, you will eliminate them and end up with a mighty pricey supper.[9]

You can cook with fresh buds from your own garden or dry them in a dehydrator. Choose mature buds, the ones ready to flower the next day – these have the most flavour, somewhere between a green bean and an asparagus stalk. Because daylilies keep sending out new buds, harvesting them either from the wild or hybrid cultivars will not affect the plant, but pick the milder, yellow varieties – the red buds are notoriously bitter. Dried lily buds can be purchased in Asian markets. When shopping, look for pale, golden buds, the paler the better. The dried buds must be rinsed and soaked from 30 to 60 minutes before cooking. Drain them, cut off any tough stem ends and use as a vegetable with pork or poultry dishes or with other vegetables in a stir fry or soup. Their earthy flavour is a traditional ingredient in Asian hot-and-sour soup and mu shu pork.

opposite: Orange daylily (*Hemerocallis fulva*). Both flowers and buds are edible.

Gigli pasta in the shape of lily flowers.

If the buds are long, cut them in half or tie in a knot to form bite-sized pieces that will stay intact when cooked. Once you become a truly enthusiastic lily chef, you can even learn how to fold a napkin to look like a lily.

Epilogue: A Journey in Shushan

❦

I have been a gardener and a writer for most of my life, but never before have the two come so close together as when I began researching this book. After tending a small rowhouse garden in Brooklyn for many years, mostly of vegetables, I was unprepared, when I moved to a farmhouse in upstate New York, for the pleasures of a country flower garden. There I inherited a perennial garden with many flower beds and several different kinds of lilies, most unknown to me. The name of this tiny village, Shushan, was also new to me, and it was only when starting the research for this book that I discovered the surprising coincidence that the name was the Hebrew word for lily. The name also appears in several books of the Hebrew Bible (Esther, Daniel and Nehemiah) as a place in ancient Persia, perhaps one where the lilies of the Song of Songs grew. The association has no particular relevance to my village of Shushan, more like rocky New England than the lush lands of the Old Testament. It was assigned at random in the early twentieth century, so the story goes, by the local postman – who did not have lilies in mind. He had grown tired of forwarding misdirected mail sent to the village, originally called East Salem, but actually addressed to several other Salems in the region. Opening a Bible, he picked a name unlike any other. A small plaque in the village centre attests to the fact that it is the only Shushan in the United States. How strange that it would find me here, writing a book about lilies.

Over time, I came to know every flower in my garden, but the lilies presented a special challenge. I was never sure where they would sprout and my trowel often split a buried bulb in half while I dug a place for another plant. Chipmunks usually got there before me, gnawing away at the fleshy bulbs. To replace them, a dear friend at Maplecrest Lilies in Maine sent me several dozen hybrid treasures as a birthday present. Before planting the bulbs in the autumn, I wrapped each one carefully in chicken wire, pricking my fingers on the stiff mesh. But in the spring my heart sank when I saw that a band of ravenous chipmunks had nibbled down the tender green shoots poking through the soil. Those that did manage to grow to full height had their flower buds nipped off just before blooming, by nocturnal deer or acrobatic chipmunks. Since then, I have learned in researching the use of lilies that the bulbs have been a favourite food of many cultures for centuries. The chipmunks and the deer have clearly brought this point home.

Armed with repellent sprays, chilli pepper and chicken wire tents, I've managed to bring several survivors to flower. Each year, their surprising bloom has stopped me in my tracks, in awe of such commanding beauty. Outsmarting the wildlife is not what gives me a thrill. I now realize, after reading about their origins and gazing at centuries-old botanical illustrations, that I have global history growing in my garden. The tall Turk's caps so loved by the deer are proof that the ancient traders carried bulbs like these from the Ottoman Empire to Vienna in the sixteenth century. The tiger lilies, whose ancestors made their first trip from China to Kew Gardens more than 200 years ago, continue to plant their future generations of tiny black bulbils in my rocky soil.

The lilies of the valley making a dense carpet over the roots of my old maple tree are just like the ones studding the green grass in the Unicorn Tapestries, woven six centuries ago, that my husband and I marvelled at in the Cloisters Museum at the Metropolitan Museum of Art, New York, several years ago. Even the orange daylilies that I thought were American natives were brought from China to Britain in the sixteenth century. I've also learned to call a little white lily by its right name, *Lilium speciosum*, and was amazed to discover from B&D

Tiger lilies in the author's garden. The downward-facing blooms with reflexed petals are also known as Turk's caps. A fixture of gardens today, they were first brought to the West from the Ottoman Empire in the 16th century.

Lilies, the passionate growers of wild lilies in Washington State, that a variety of this Japanese native, *L. speciosum rubrum* 'Uchida', was the subject of horticultural heroism in the Second World War. It was protected by a Japanese man who defied the orders of the imperial Japanese government to destroy his ornamental garden and plant potatoes for the army. He hid the bulbs and they now grace gardens like mine all over the world. When they bloom next spring, I will think of Uchida Hirotaka's bravery – his determined refusal to destroy beauty. And if my sole water lily consents to send one pink bloom up again next summer, I will think not only of Claude Monet, who would laugh at my tiny pond, but also of Joseph Paxton, who saw a vision of the Crystal Palace in the ribbed leaves of the giant water lily of the Amazon, of which just one leaf would cover my pond.

I've also learned of a lily hybrid called 'Shuksan', created in 1924 at a research station in Bellingham, Washington, not far from Mount Shuksan. In his book on lilies, Brian Mathew extols Shuksan as 'a magnificent vigorous lily with large orange-yellow flowers conspicuously blotched dull red'.[1] Its creator, David Griffiths, may have known that the name was also the Hebrew word for lily, but I wonder if he had ever heard of Shushan, New York. In any case, as I write this reflection on lilies, in the dead of a New York winter, I am making a note to add the magnificent 'Shuksan' to my list of lilies to plant in my garden next year, well guarded against chipmunks and deer. Writing and gardening in Shushan has been my journey of discovery and creation. I hope this book will be the same for my readers, wherever they may garden.

Timeline

≈

c. 2500–1450 BC	Images of lilies are painted on wall murals and engraved in jewellery and pottery in the ancient Minoan civilization on the Greek islands of the Aegean
c. 2500–800 BC	Ancient Egyptians engrave lilies and water lilies on tombs and use them in religious ceremonies and to make perfumes
c. 500–AD 450	The Romans spread the Madonna lily throughout their empire The poet Virgil names it *candidum*, shining white
c. 200 BC	Chinese scholars compile the first extant text referring to lilies, the *Divine Husbandman's Classic of Materia Medica*
AD 493	Clovis I converts to Christianity, the legendary beginning of the French monarchy's adoption of the fleur-de-lis as its heraldic emblem
c. 700	The Venerable Bede cites the white lily as the emblem of the Virgin Mother's purity, 'the pure white petals signifying her spotless body and the golden anthers her soul glowing with heavenly light'
c. 800	Charlemagne issues *Capitulare de villis*, a list of plants, headed by lilies and roses, to be grown in every town of the Holy Roman Empire
c. 900–60	The cultivation of lily bulbs for food is documented in the Chinese agricultural treatise *Compendium of Essential Tasks for the Four Seasons*

c. 1400–1600	The Madonna lily is the pre-eminent symbol in countless Renaissance paintings of the Annunciation
c. 1554–62	The Holy Roman Emperor's ambassador to Constantinople introduces Turkish bulbs of lilies, tulips and other 'exotic' flowers to the Western world The orange daylily arrives in Britain from China
1632–54	Red lilies are engraved on the walls of the Taj Mahal and on the tombs of Shah Jahan and his wife
1691	The orange lily, *L. bulbiferum* var. *croceum*, becomes a symbol of the Protestant Orangemen celebrating the victory of William of Orange over Irish Catholics who had supported James II
1736	Philadelphia farmer John Bertram sends bulbs of the American lily, *L. superbum*, from the colonies to Britain, where it becomes the subject of paintings by leading botanical artists
1776	The Swedish plant explorer Carl Peter Thunberg discovers *L. longiflorum*, later known as the Easter lily, on the Ryukyu Islands of southern Japan
1804	William Kerr sends the tiger lily, *L. lancifolium*, from China to Kew Gardens in London
1849	Joseph Paxton succeeds in coaxing the giant water lily, *Victoria amazonica*, to flower in England and it becomes his inspiration for the design of the Crystal Palace
1862	The British nurseryman John Veitch introduces the 'Queen of Lilies', *L. auratum*, a Japanese discovery, to Britain, causing a horticultural sensation
c. 1870–1895	The white lily becomes an emblem of the Aesthetic Movement and the signature flower of Oscar Wilde
1896	Claude Monet begins painting the water lilies in his ponds at Giverny, the focus of his work for the next 30 years until his death in 1926

1903	'Chinese' Wilson discovers the regal lily in the wilds of China and becomes the most famous exotic flower collector of his day
1920s	Georgia O'Keeffe's psycho-sexual calla lily paintings create a sensation
1941	Jan de Graaff creates the hybrid lily 'Enchantment', changing the lily's reputation from a horticultural challenge to one of the most popular garden flowers
1970s	Judith Freeman, a pioneer in embryo culture, creates 'Tiger Babies', one of the first 'test tube' hybrids between true lily species once thought impossible to cross
1978	Leslie Woodriff creates the hybrid 'Stargazer', the first widely successful Oriental lily hybrid and one of the most popular types of lilies
2010	'Lilytopia', the largest lily exhibition ever mounted in North America, is held at Longwood Gardens in Pennsylvania, one of the nation's largest botanical gardens
2011	The world's largest display of lilies is presented at Keukenhof Gardens in Lisse, Netherlands

References

❧

Introduction

1 Susan Vreeland, *Clara and Mr Tiffany* (New York, 2011), p. 273.
2 Colette, 'Flowers and Fruits', in *My Favorite Plant*, ed. Jamaica Kincaid (New York, 1998), p. 65.
3 B&D Lilies, 'Knowledge Base of Wild Lilies' (2008), at www.bdlillies.com (accessed 12 July 2012).
4 Jamaica Kincaid, *My Garden Book* (New York, 1999), p. 67.
5 Colette, 'Flowers and Fruits', p. 65.
6 Cited in James Moore, 'The Pale Beauty of Priceless Flowers: Market and Meaning in O'Keeffe's Calla Lily Paintings', in *Georgia O'Keeffe and the Calla Lily in American Art, 1860–1940*, ed. Barbara Buhler Lynes (New Haven, CT, 2002), p. 45.

1 A Lily by Any Other Name

1 Wilfrid Blunt and Sandra Raphael, *The Illustrated Herbal* (London, 1979), p. 14.
2 Jack Goody, *The Culture of Flowers* (Cambridge, 1993), p. 350.
3 Birkhard Bilger, 'The Great Oasis', *New Yorker* (19–26 December 2011), p. 114.
4 Charlie Kroell, email to the author, 25 November 2012.
5 Charlie Kroell, email to the author, 28 November 2012.
6 Shirley Sherwood and Martyn Rix, *Treasures of Botanical Art* (London, 2008), p. 152.
7 Simon Kelly, *Monet's Water Lilies: The Agapanthus Triptych* (St Louis, MO, 2011), pp. 14–15.
8 Ibid., pp. 17–18.

2 From the Ice Age to the Modern Age

1 Alice M. Coats, *Flowers and their Histories* (London, 1968), p. 142.
2 Penelope Hobhouse, *Plants in Garden History* (London, 1997), p. 16.

3　Cited in Jack Goody, *The Culture of Flowers* (Cambridge, 1993), p. 64.

4　Hobhouse, *Plants in Garden History*, p. 70.

5　Stephen G. Haw, *The Lilies of China* (Portland, OR, 1986), p. 15.

6　Goody, *Culture of Flowers*, p. 352.

7　Cited in Hobhouse, *Plants in Garden History*, p. 96.

8　John McClintock and James Strong, *Cyclopaedia of Biblical, Theological and Ecclesiastical Literature*, vol. V (Cambridge, MA, 1896), p. 432.

9　Hobhouse, *Plants in Garden History*, pp. 40, 66–7.

10　Ibid., p. 21.

11　Goody, *Culture of Flowers*, p. 184.

12　Haw, *Lilies of China*, p. 51.

13　Coats, *Flowers and their Histories*, p. 145.

14　Leonard Perry, 'Easter Lilies', at University of Vermont, Department of Plant and Soil Science website, http://pss.uvm.edu (last accessed 12 July 2012).

15　Pamela McGeorge, *Lilies* (Auckland, 2004), p. 62.

16　Haw, *Lilies of China*, p. 54.

17　Brian Mathew, *Lilies: A Romantic History with a Guide to Cultivation* (London, 1993), p. 47.

18　Alexander Wallace, *Notes on Lilies and their Culture* (London, 1879), p. 1.

19　Coats, *Flowers and their Histories*, p. 148.

20　Cited in McGeorge, *Lilies*, p. 49.

21　Mathew, *Lilies*, p. 49.

22　B&D Lilies, 'Knowledge Base of Wild Lilies' (2008), at www.bdlillies.com (accessed 12 July 2012).

23　Brent Elliott, *Flora: An Illustrated History of the Garden Flower* (Willowdale, Ontario, 2001), p. 34.

24　Coats, *Flowers and their Histories*, p. 148.

25　Patti Hagan, *Horticulture*, cited in *New York Times*, Obituary for Jan de Graff, 9 August 1989.

26　Brian Bergman, 'Comments on "A Revolution in Lilies", Presented by Peter Schenk (2011)', *North American Lily Society Quarterly Bulletin*, LXVI/4 (December 2012), p. 10.

27　Cited in McGeorge, *Lilies,* p. 68.

28　B&D Lilies, 'Knowledge Base of Wild Lilies' (2008), at www.bdlilies.com (accessed 28 November 2012).

29　Charlie Kroell, email to the author, 1 December 2012.

3 A Lily in Every Garden

1　Penelope Hobhouse, *Plants in Garden History* (London, 1997), p. 11.

2　Cited ibid., p. 12.

3　Derek Clifford, *A History of Garden Design* (New York, 1963), p. 24.

4　Ibid., p. 28.

5 Hobhouse, *Plants in Garden History*, p. 30.
6 Cited in Clifford, *A History of Garden Design*, p. 30.
7 Hobhouse, *Plants in Garden History*, pp. 58–9.
8 Ibid., p. 70.
9 Ibid.
10 Ibid., p. 86.
11 Ibid., p. 73.
12 Cited in Marina Heilmeyer, *The Language of Flowers* (New York, 2006), p. 10.
13 Hobhouse, *Plants in Garden History*, p. 82.
14 Ibid., p. 137.
15 Ibid.
16 Gill Saunders, *Picturing Plants* (Los Angeles and London, 1995), p. 41.
17 Hobhouse, *Plants in Garden History*, pp. 144–5.
18 Clifford, *A History of Garden Design*, pp. 65–6.
19 Saunders, *Picturing Plants*, p. 52.
20 Clifford, *A History of Garden Design*, p. 80.
21 Hobhouse, *Plants in Garden History*, pp. 186–7.
22 Ibid., p. 137.
23 Ibid., p. 205.
24 Ibid., p. 202.
25 Ibid., p. 231.
26 John Fisk Allen, *Victoria Regia; or, The Great Water Lily of America* (Boston, MA, 1854).
27 Ibid.
28 Ibid.
29 At www.longwoodgardens.org (accessed 8 December 2012).
30 At www.keukenhof.nl (accessed 8 December 2012).

4 Picturing the Lily

1 Gill Saunders, *Picturing Plants* (Los Angeles and London, 1995), p. 18.
2 Cited in Wilfrid Blunt and Sandra Raphael, *The Illustrated Herbal* (London, 1979), p. 17.
3 Ibid., p. 57.
4 Ibid., p. 134.
5 Nancy Keeler, *Gardens in Perpetual Bloom* (Boston, MA, 2009), pp. 9–10.
6 Shirley Sherwood and Martyn Rix, *Treasures of Botanical Art* (London, 2008), p. 54.
7 Cited in Saunders, *Picturing Plants*, p. 89.
8 Andrea Wulf, *The Brother Gardeners* (New York, 2008), p. 257.
9 Alice M. Coats, *The Book of Flowers* (New York, 1973), p. 17.
10 John Fisk Allen, *Victoria Regia; or, The Great Water Lily of America* (Boston, MA, 1854).
11 Ibid.
12 Keeler, *Gardens in Perpetual Bloom*, p. 120.

13 Alice M. Coats, *Treasury of Flowers* (London, 1975), p. 9.
14 *The Botanical Artist: Journal of the American Society of Botanical Artists*, XVII/3 (September 2011), p. 23.
15 Sherwood and Rix, *Treasures of Botanical Art*, p. 12.
16 At www.lisaholley.com (accessed 7 December 2012).

5 Milk, Blood and Sex

1 Rose-Marie Hagen and Rainer Hagen, *What Great Paintings Say* (Los Angeles, 2000), pp. 189–91.
2 'Jacopo Tintoretto, *The Origin of the Milky Way*', at website of National Gallery, London, www.nationalgallery.org.uk (accessed 4 July 2012).
3 Lillian M. Fisher, *Kateri Tekakwitha: The Lily of the Mohawks* (Boston, MA, 1995), pp. 120–22.
4 Mariann Burke, *Re-imagining Mary: A Journey through Art to the Feminine Self* (Carmel, CA, 2009), p. 66.
5 Marina Heilmeyer, *The Language of Flowers* (New York, 2006), p. 48.
6 Debra Mancoff, *Flora Symbolica: Flowers in Pre-Raphaelite Art* (New York, 2003), p. 58.
7 Bobby I. Ward, *Contemplation upon Flowers: Garden Plants in Myth and Literature* (Portland, OR, 2005), p. 174.
8 'Forest Legends: St Leonard and the Dragon', at www.friendsof-stleonardsforest.org.uk (accessed 4 July 2012).
9 Charles M. Skinner, *Myths and Legends of Flowers, Trees, Fruits and Plants in All Ages and in All Climes* (Philadelphia, 1911).
10 Claire O'Rush, *The Enchanted Garden* (New York, 2000), p. 80.
11 Mancoff, *Flora Symbolica*, p. 38.

6 As Pure as a Lily

1 Jack Goody, *The Culture of Flowers* (Cambridge, 1993), p. 88.
2 Ibid., p. 85.
3 Cited in Alice M. Coats, *Flowers and their Histories* (London, 1968), p. 142.
4 Goody, *Culture of Flowers*, p. 157.
5 Derek Clifford, *A History of Garden Design* (New York, 1963), p. 19.
6 Penelope Hobhouse, *Plants in Garden History* (London, 1997), p. 138.
7 Judith Farr, *The Passion of Emily Dickinson* (Cambridge, MA, 1992), p. 39.
8 *Drawings and Studies by Sir Edward Burne-Jones*, exh. cat., Burlington Fine Arts Club, London (1899), p. vii.
9 'Kimono with Carp, Water Lilies, and Morning Glories (Japan) (2006.73.2)', in *Heilbrunn Timeline of Art History*, New York: The Metropolitan Museum of Art, 2000.
10 Cited in Charles C. Eldredge, 'Calla Moderna: "Such a Strange Flower"', in *Georgia O'Keeffe and the Calla Lily in American Art, 1860–1940*, ed. Barbara Buhler Lynes (New Haven, CT, 2002), p. 12.

11 Cited in Simon Kelly, *Monet's Water Lilies: The Agapanthus Triptych* (St Louis, MO, 2011), p. 17.

12 Cited ibid., p. 29.

13 Cited ibid., p. 13.

7 The Sexiest Flower

1 Jack Goody, *The Culture of Flowers* (Cambridge, 1993), p. 5.

2 Andrea Wulf, *The Brother Gardeners* (New York, 2008), p. 59.

3 Elizabeth Anne Jones, *Awaken to Healing Fragrance: The Power of Essential Oil Therapy* (Berkeley, CA, 1999). pp. 3, 23 and 91. Lilies and many other flowers were distilled and mixed in perfumes prepared for royal women.

4 Goody, *Culture of Flowers*, p. 204.

5 Judith Farr, *The Gardens of Emily Dickinson* (Cambridge, MA, 2004), p. 31.

6 Judith Farr, *The Passion of Emily Dickinson* (Cambridge, MA, 1992), p. 38.

7 Ibid., p. 39.

8 Ibid., p. 168.

9 Daniel Mendelshon, 'The Two Oscar Wildes', *New York Review of Books* (10 October 2002).

10 Department of Ecology, State of Washington, 'Non-invasive Freshwater Plants', at www.ecy.was.gov (accessed 26 April 2012)

11 Charles Eldredge, 'Calla Moderna: Such a Strange Flower', in *Georgia O'Keeffe and the Calla Lily in American Art, 1860–1940*, ed. Barbara Buhler Lynes (New Haven, CT, 2002), p. 18.

12 Ibid., p. 25.

13 James Moore, 'The Pale Beauty of Priceless Flowers: Market and Meaning in O'Keeffe's Calla Lily Paintings', in *Georgia O'Keeffe and the Calla Lily*, ed. Lynes, p. 51.

14 Luis-Martin Lozano and Juan Rafael Coronel Rivera, *Diego Rivera: The Complete Murals* (Berlin, 2008), p. 567.

15 Deborah A. Levinson, 'Robert Mapplethorpe's Extraordinary Vision', review of 'The Perfect Moment' Exhibition for the Washington Project for the Arts at the Institute for Contemporary Art, Washington, DC, 1989, *The Tech* (Cambridge, MA, 1990).

8 Matters of Life and Death

1 Jack Goody, *The Culture of Flowers* (Cambridge, 1993), p. 67.

2 Debra Mancoff, *Flora Symbolica: Flowers in Pre-Raphaelite Art* (New York, 2003), p. 36.

3 James Moore, 'The Pale Beauty of Priceless Flowers', in *Georgia O'Keeffe and the Calla Lily in American Art, 1860–1940*, ed. Barbara Buhler Lynes (New Haven, CT, 2002), p. 55.

4 Ibid., p. 13.

5 Simon Kelly, *Monet's Water Lilies: The Agapanthus Triptych* (St Louis, MO, 2011), p. 27.

9 Always Entertaining

1 Programme notes for *The Importance of Being Earnest* at People's Light & Theatre Company, Malvern, PA, June 1993.
2 Debra Mancoff, *Flora Symbolica: Flowers in Pre-Raphaelite Art* (New York, 2003), p. 84.
3 Ibid.
4 Pliny the Elder, *The Natural History*, trans. John Bostock and H. T. Riley (1855), www.perseus.edu; translation of 1601, cited in Brian Mathew, *Lillies: A Romantic History with a Guide to Cultivation* (London, 1993), p. 21.
5 Cited in Alice M. Coats, *Flowers and their Histories* (London, 1968), p. 142.

10 A Lily a Day Keeps the Doctor Away

1 Stephen G. Haw, *The Lilies of China* (Portland, OR, 1986), p. 43.
2 Jack Goody, *The Culture of Flowers* (Cambridge, 1993), p. 370; Alice M. Coats, *Flowers and their Histories* (London, 1968), p. 114; Peter Gail, *The Delightful Delicious Daylily*, 2nd edn (Cleveland, OH, 1995), p. 16.
3 Haw, *Lilies of China*, p. 43.
4 Coats, *Flowers and their Histories*, p. 311.
5 Wilfrid Blunt and Sandra Raphael, *The Illustrated Herbal* (London, 1979), p. 17.
6 Coats, *Flowers and their Histories*, p. 56.
7 Ibid., p. 57.
8 Alice M. Coats, *The Treasury of Flowers* (London, 1975), p. 116.
9 In large doses, sea squill bulbs can be highly toxic and have been used in rat poison; www.bulbsociety.org (accessed 12 July 2012).
10 Brian Matthew, *Lilies: A Romantic History with a Guide to Cultivation* (London, 1993), p. 14.
11 Palomar College, San Marcos, CA, 'Soap Lilies in California', at www.palomar.edu (accessed 12 July 2012).
12 Haw, *Lilies of China*, p. 43.
13 Marina Heilmeyer, *The Language of Flowers* (New York, 2006), p. 7.
14 Clare Cooper Marcus, *Healing Gardens: Therapeutic Benefits and Design Recommendations* (Hoboken, NJ, 1999), p. 2.

11 Lilies on Your Plate

1 'Yellow Martagon Lily, *Lilium pomponium*', at www.aboutflowers.org (accessed 12 July 2012).
2 USDA Forest Service, 'Celebrating Wildflowers: Intermountain Region. Camas Prairie', at http://www.fs.fed.us/wildflowers (accessed 12 July 2012).
3 Cited in Stephen G. Haw, *The Lilies of China* (Portland, OR, 1986), p. 47.
4 Ibid., pp. 48–9.
5 Jack Goody, *The Culture of Flowers* (Cambridge, 1993), p. 181.
6 Jean-Anthelme Brillat-Savarin, *The Physiology of Taste*, trans. M.F.K. Fisher (New York, 1946), p. 357.

7 Conversation with Craig Barnes, Slate Hill Farm Daylilies, Salem, New York.
8 Peter Gail, *The Delightful Delicious Daylily*, 2nd end (Cleveland, OH, 1989), p. 27.
9 Ibid., p. 21.

Epilogue

1 Brian Mathew, *Lilies: A Romantic History with a Guide to Cultivation* (London, 1993), p. 41.

Further Reading

✺

Blunt, Wilfrid, and Sandra Raphael, *The Illustrated Herbal* (London, 1979)
Clifford, Derek, *A History of Garden Design* (New York, 1963)
Coats, Alice M., *The Book of Flowers* (London, 1973)
—, *Flowers and their Histories* (London, 1968)
—, *The Treasury of Flowers* (London, 1975)
Elliott, Brent, *Flora: An Illustrated History of the Garden Flower* (Willowdale, Ontario, 2001)
Farr, Judith, *The Gardens of Emily Dickinson* (Cambridge, MA, 2004)
—, *The Passion of Emily Dickinson* (Cambridge, MA, 1992)
Fisher, Lillian M., *Kateri Tekakwitha: The Lily of the Mohawks* (Boston, MA, 1995)
Gail, Peter A., *The Delightful Delicious Daylily* (Cleveland, OH, 1995)
Goody, Jack, *The Culture of Flowers* (Cambridge, 1993)
Haw, Stephen, *The Lilies of China* (Portland, OR, 1986)
Heilmeyer, Marina, *The Language of Flowers* (New York, 2006)
Hobhouse, Penelope, *Plants in Garden History: An Illustrated History of Plants and their Influence on Garden Styles from Ancient Egypt to the Present Day* (London, 1997)
Jekyll, Gertrude, *Lilies for English Gardens: A Guide for Amateurs* (London, 1903)
Keeler, Nancy, *Gardens in Perpetual Bloom: Botanical Illustration in Europe and America, 1600–1850* (Boston, MA, 2009)
Kelly, Simon, with Mary Schafer and Johanna Bernstein, *Monet's Water Lilies: The Agapanthus Triptych* (St Louis, MO, 2011)
Kincaid, Jamaica, ed., *My Favorite Plant* (New York, 1998)
—, *My Garden Book* (New York, 1999)
Lynes, Barbara Buhler, ed., *Georgia O'Keeffe and the Calla Lily in American Art, 1860–1940* (New Haven, CT, 2002)
McGeorge, Pamela, *Lilies* (Auckland, 2004)
McRae, Edward Austin, *Lilies: A Guide for Growers and Collectors* (Portland, OR, 1998)
Mancoff, Debra, *Flora Symbolica: Flowers in Pre-Raphaelite Art* (New York, 2003)
Mathew, Brian, *Lilies: A Romantic History with a Guide to Cultivation* (London, 1993)
Saunders, Gill, *Picturing Plants: An Analytical History of Botanical Illustration* (Los Angeles and London, 1995)

Sherwood, Shirley, and Martyn Rix, *Treasures of Botanical Art* (London, 2008)
Wallace, Alexander, *Notes on Lilies and their Culture* (London, 1879)
Ward, Bobby I., *A Contemplation upon Flowers: Garden Plants in Myth and Literature* (Portland, OR, 2005)
Wulf, Andrea, *The Brother Gardeners: Botany, Empire and the Birth of an Obsession* (New York, 2008).

Associations and Websites

❧

AMERICAN HEMEROCALLIS SOCIETY
Quarterly publication and additional information about daylilies
www.daylilies.org

B&D LILIES
Port Townsend, Washington
True lily bulbs by mail order, including hybrid and species lilies
www.bdlilies.com

BROOKLYN BOTANIC GARDEN
Brooklyn, New York City
Extensive public gardens and greenhouses, including scenic water lily pools
www.bbg.org

DAYLILY LAY
St Peter's, Missouri
Mail order daylilies and seeds
www.daylilylay.com

KEUKENHOF
Lisse, The Netherlands
Open-air gardens of flowering bulbs, including a vast lily show and annual
lily parade
www.keukenhof.nl

THE LILY GARDEN
Vancouver, Washington
True lily bulbs, including unusual hybrids by the geneticist Judith Freeman
www.thelilygarden.com

THE LILY NOOK
Neepawa, Manitoba, Canada
True lily hybrids and species bulbs by mail order
www.lilynook.mb.ca

LONGWOOD GARDENS
Kennett Square, Pennsylvania
More than 1,000 acres of public gardens of all kinds, including the annual
Lilytopia festival
www.longwoodgardens.org

MAPLECREST LILIES
East Parsonsfield, Maine
True lily hybrid bulbs and fresh cut stems by mail order
www.maplecrestlilies.com

NORTH AMERICAN LILY SOCIETY
Publications, seed exchange and information about true lilies
www.lilies.org

ROYAL HORTICULTURAL SOCIETY LILY GROUP
Publications, seeds and information about true lilies
www.rhslilygroup.org

SHIRLEY SHERWOOD GALLERY OF BOTANICAL ART AT KEW GARDENS
London, uk
The only gallery devoted solely to botanical art, located within the famous
Kew Gardens. Historic and contemporary prints of all kinds, including lilies
www.kew.org

SLATE HILL FARM DAYLILIES
Salem, New York
Mail order daylilies and direct sales at the farm. An official American
Hemerocallis Society Display Garden open at weekends during July
and August
www.slatehillfarm.com

Acknowledgements

Personally and professionally, the art historian Debra Mancoff was my inspiration for this book. She urged me to write it and provided support and suggestions to get me started on the right track. Her extensive body of work was a valuable source of knowledge on gardens and art. I also was fortunate to have the enthusiastic support and advice about true lilies from my lifelong friend, Memarie Christoforo, of Maplecrest Lilies in East Parsonsfield, Maine. Charlie Kroell opened my eyes to the beauty and extraordinary diversity of true lily species, graciously contributing his time, personal experience and extensive knowledge as a devoted *Lilium* collector and breeder. His photos and those shared by his colleagues from the North American Lily Society, including Joe Nemmer, Rimmer de Vries and Stephanie and David Sims, provided rare views of true lilies usually seen only in the wild or in the carefully cultivated gardens of horticulturalists. I wish we had had the space to include them all. The daylily grower and hyridizer Michael Bouman of DayLily Lay and the American Hemerocallis Society was equally kind in sharing his knowledge and beautiful photos. AHS members Craig and Mary Barnes provided first-hand information about raising, breeding and even eating daylilies at their beautiful Slate Hill Farm in Salem, New York. I am grateful to all of these lily experts, yet take full responsibility for any lily inaccuracies. In searching for poems about lilies, I could not have found better help than the services kindly provided by Lee Briccetti, executive director of Poets House in New York City, and her able intern, Kimberly Grabowski. The talented photographer Larry Racioppo generously shared his amazing photo of the *Giglio*, the lily festival in Williamsburg, Brooklyn. Jeffrey Moser, an experimental media artist, expertly tweaked my amateur photos into the proper format for reproduction. Thanks also to friends and neighbours: Barbara Villet for information about the sea squill's use in cough medicine, and Anita Witten for the tasty tidbit about Brillat-Savarin's lily pastilles. Above all, thanks to my husband, Charlie, who – although not a gardener – read every word I wrote about lilies with insight and enthusiasm, and helped my work grow from an idea to a book.

Photo Acknowledgements

࿔

The author and publishers wish to express their thanks to the below sources of illustrative material and/or permission to reproduce it. Locations of some artworks are also given below.

Photo Laure Albin-Guillot/Roger-Viollet, courtesy Rex Features: p. 125; photo © AntiMartina/2012 iStock International Inc.: p. 197; Ashmolean Museum, Oxford: p. 34; photos author: pp. 30, 45, 47, 201; © 2013 Banco de México Diego Rivera Frida Kahlo Museums Trust, Mexico, D.F./DACS: p. 151; Basilica di San Domenico, Siena: p. 124; photo Brendan Beirne/Rex Features: p. 136; photo Nigel R. Barklie/Rex Features: p. 18; photoBigstock-Photo: p. 190; Birmingham Museums and Art Gallery: p. 108; Bodleian Library, Oxford: pp. 35, 82; photo Michael Bouman: p. 24; photos Jacques Boyer/Roger-Viollet, courtesy Rex Features: pp. 28 (top), 189; photo Maurice-Louis Branger/Roger-Viollet, courtesy Rex Features: p. 28 (foot); British Library, London: p. 117; British Museum, London (photos © The Trustees of the British Museum): pp. 9, 12, 38, 42, 78, 88, 109, 110, 121, 126, 132, 140; photos © The Trustees of the British Museum: 87, 99, 114, 122, 123, 129 (left), 145, 156, 172 (foot); photo Pierre Choumoff/Roger-Viollet, courtesy Rex Features: p. 32 (top); photos elwynn: pp. 190, 194; photos courtesy Everett Collection/Rex Features: pp. 147, 178; photo Michael Friedel/Rex Features: p. 158; photo Anders Good/Rex Features: p. 27; photo Paul Grover/Rex Features: pp. 74–5; photo Krestine Havermann/Daily Mail/Rex Features: p. 163; photo Charles Huralt/Roger-Viollet, courtesy Rex Features: p. 139; photo © 2012 iStock International Inc.: p. 194; photo © Pierre Jahan/Roger-Viollet, courtesy Rex Features: p. 168; photo Charlie Kroell: p. 21; photo Lehtikuva OY/Rex Features: p. 32 (foot); photo © Léon et Lévy/Roger-Viollet, courtesy Rex Features: p. 119; Library of Congress, Washington, DC: pp. 8, 11, 46, 47, 128, 134, 135 (foot); Manchester Art Gallery: p. 105; photo © Henri Manuel/Roger-Viollet, courtesy Rex Features: p. 166; from Mara Sibylla Merian, *Histoire des Insectes de l'Europe, Deffinée d'après nature & expliquée par Marie Sibille Merian: Où l'on traite de la Generation & des différentes Metamorphoses des Chenilles, Vers, Papillons, Mouches & autres Insectes; et des Plantes, des Fleurs & des Fruits dont ils se nourrissent...* (Amsterdam, 1730): p. 93; photo © miralex/2012 iStock International Inc.: p. 31; photo Jeffrey Moser: p. 113; photo ©

Musée Carnavalet, Paris/Roger-Viollet, courtesy Rex Features: p. 172 (top);
Musée Malraux, Le Havre: p. 167; National Gallery, London: p. 96; photo Joe
Nemmer: p. 22; © Georgia O'Keeffe Museum/DACS, 2012: p. 149; Museum of
Fine Arts, Boston: p. 149; private collection: p. 151; photos Rex Features 72, 169;
Rijksmuseum, Amsterdam: p. 119; photos © Roger-Viollet, courtesy Rex Features:
pp. 56, 91, 111, 118, 124, 131, 154, 165, 187; photo Edwin Rosskam: p. 47; Santa Maria
della Rotonda (The Pantheon), Rome: p. 13; photo Solent News/Rex Features:
pp. 76-77; The Terra Foundation for American Art: p. 135 (top); Sheila Terry/
Robert Harding/Rex Features: p. 62; from Robert Thompson, *The Gardener's Assistant: Practical and Scientific. A Guide to the Formation and Management of The Kitchen, Fruit and Flower Garden, and the Cultivation of Conservatory, Green-house, and Stove Plants, with a Copious Calendar of Gardening Operations* (London, 1859): p. 87; from Christoph Jakob
Trew, *Plantae Selectae quorum imagines ad exemplaria naturalia Londini in hortis curiosorum nutrita...* (Nuremberg, 1750-77): p. 85; Victoria & Albert Museum, London
(photos courtesy V&A Images): pp. 14, 25, 133, 170, 177; photo courtesy V&A
Images: p. 10; Walker Art Gallery, Liverpool: p. 107; Werner Forman Archive/Iraq
Museum, Baghdad: p. 39; Werner Forman Archive/Musée du Louvre, Paris: p. 182;
Werner Forman Archive/private collection: p. 129 (right); Werner Forman
Archive/N. J. Saunders: p. 36; Werner Forman Archive/State University Library,
Leiden Oriental Collection: p. 80.

Index